THE NEVER ENDING SEASON

The Cookbook
Of Missouri

LEISURE
TIME
PUBLISHING,
INC.

Published by Missouri 4-H Foundation, Columbia, Missouri, in association with Leisure Time Publishing, a division of Heritage Worldwide, Inc., Dallas, Texas.

Publisher:	Rodney L. Dockery
General Manager & Editorial Director:	Caleb Pirtle III
Regional Publishing Director:	Suzanne Breitbach
Project Coordinator:	Betty Miser
Production Coordinator:	Kathy Hazel
Production Manager:	Vickie Craig
Marketing Director:	Diane Luther
Text:	Diane Luther and Kitty Smith
Proofreading:	Bruce H. Deatherage, Ph.D.
Photography:	Tom Nagel, Randall Hyman, Farmland Foods, Inc., Missouri Soybean Merchandising Council & Missouri Department of Natural Resources

Cover photograph courtesy of Mid-America Dairymen, Inc.

Carthage Court House photograph courtesy of Ott Food Products.

Recipes appearing in *The Never Ending Season* were provided to Leisure Time Publishing by food manufacturers and food processors throughout Missouri. In addition, the Missouri Department of Agriculture gave Leisure Time permission to use recipes from its Agri-Missouri cookbook. We respect the time and effort that each company and the Department of Agriculture took in the creation of these favorite recipes, and we chose to include them in the book in much the same form as they were received by Leisure Time.

However, in order to create a broader awareness of the many great products made in the state and to benefit you in your efforts to proudly support those products, Leisure Time Publishing has taken the liberty of customizing ingredients in the recipes with Missouri-made brands.

Printed by:
Heritage Worldwide, Inc.
9029 Directors Row
Dallas, Texas 75247
Telephone: (214) 630-4300

First Printing

Manufactured in the United States of America.

Contents

Foreword

The Missouri 4-H Program has more than 75 years of history of contribution to the development of Missouri Youth.

Four-H has grown from an organization dedicated to developing youth in the primarily rural environment of 1914, to serving the total community of today.

- Missouri 4-H Programs Involve Over 135,000 Youths
    - 39% urban (over 50,000 population)
    - 48% town (under 50,000 population)
    - 13% farm
- Local clubs featuring family-oriented experiential education (30,000)
- Science and technology education in school classrooms (100,000)
- After-School Child Care programs (2,000)
- Collaborative efforts in substance abuse, teen suicide, teen pregnancy and other destructive issues (3,000)

The Missouri Food Industry parallels the development of 4-H. As a major employer in urban areas, it provides a large portion of the Missouri economy, and is involved in the issues that face the families it employs and the neighborhoods it serves.

"The Never Ending Season" is dedicated to the principle that Missouri has tremendous pride as a state and that Missourians proudly support their own when adequately informed.

The food manufacturers featured in this book have underwritten its development costs to provide the information necessary for Missouri cooks to make informed choices.

"The Never Ending Season" was a vision of Suzanne Breitbach of Leisure Time Publishing. Missouri 4-H thanks the Missouri Department of Agriculture, particularly Mark Russell, Debbie Constanzo and Sarah Vandiver, and Ronnie Alewel and Jerry Shapiro of the Missouri Food Processors Association for their hard work, support and encouragement.

We are grateful for the endorsement of the Missouri Chamber of Commerce Agriculture Committee chaired by Elaine Osborn.

The creative genius of Caleb Pirtle and his staff has brought to life the many stories, histories and flavors of Missouri.

In particular, we recognize the sponsors who have contributed financially to make this project, and the many programs for Missouri youth that result from this effort, possible.

Diamond Level

    Ott Food Products Co., Carthage

Gold Level

    Boyle's Famous Corned Beef Co., Kansas City

    Farmland Foods, Inc., Kansas City

    Hammons Products Co., Stockton

    Hudson Foods, Inc., Springfield

    PET, Inc., St. Louis

    Seitz Foods, Inc., St. Joseph

    Wilson Foods, Marshall

Silver Level

    Andy's Seasonings, St. Louis

    MFA, Inc., Columbia

    Mid-America Dairymen, Springfield

    Missouri Farm Bureau Federation, Jefferson City

    Missouri Soybean Merchandising Council,
     Jefferson City

Bronze Level

    Aunt Nene's Specialty Foods, Lucerne

    Associated Electric Cooperative, Inc., Springfield

    Central Dairy Co., Jefferson City

    Flavors of the Heartland, Columbia

    Lucia's Pizza Co., Kirkwood

    Missouri Cattlewomen's Association, Holliday

    Morningland Dairy, Mountain View

Ozark Country Foods, Osage Beach
Petrofsky's Bakery Products, Maryland Heights
Schnuck Baking Co., St. Louis
Stone Hill Winery, Hermann
The Berry Connection & Steinbaugh Berry Farm,
  Springfield
Vess Beverages, St. Louis
Volpi and Company, Inc., St. Louis

A special thanks is also extended for the special coverage provided by the following magazines (in order of circulation):

Magazine	Circulation
Missouri State Fair Tabloid	1,300,000
Rural Missouri	337,500
Missouri Alumnus	263,716
Farm Bureau News	70,000
Missouri Ruralist	70,000
Today's Farmer	43,000
Missouri Beef Cattleman	6,000
Missouri Pork Producer	5,000
Missouri Farm	5,000
Missouri Grocer	1,700

I trust you will enjoy the stories, recipes and the many 'flavors' of Missouri found in "The Never Ending Season." I know thousands of Missouri youth appreciate your support!

Sincerely,

Konrad L. Heid
Chairman, Board of Trustees
Missouri 4-H Foundation

Leon A. Moon
President
Missouri 4-H Foundation

A Legacy

Missouri, sometimes stubborn, cantankerous, is a proud land, a peaceful land whose legacy is the spirit of its people, the promise of its good earth.

The broad, timbered shoulders of the Ozarks reach toward the clouds, and an old timer adjusts the brim of his cap as he narrows his eyes and says, "If you don't cross the ridge, then you won't get lost." It is sound advice that was given him by his mother a long time ago. And she was right. He has never left home. He has never been lost.

The gentle, rolling farmscapes are patchwork colors of greens and browns, a stark contrast between crops and freshly-plowed fields, sometimes golden in the last glow of sundown. For generations, men and women both have cast their hopes with the soil of the heartland, and, in older times, they had only the hand-me-down wisdom of backwood philosophers to guide them during their planting seasons.

"If you soak watermelon seeds in sweet milk overnight before planting them, it'll make your melons sweeter," says one.

"Never plant your beans till after you've heard the first whippoorwill's cry." says another.

And the advice is never ending.

"Cucumber seeds must be planted before sunup on May 1 to protect the vines against insects."

"Cabbage needs to be planted on Saint Valentine's Day. But if it falls on Sunday, you've got to get up and plant it before sunup so's nobody'll think you're bein' disrespectful to the Sabbath."

"If you drive nails into peach trees, then you can keep the peaches from falling off the limbs before they are ripe."

"The best time to plant corn is when the oak leaves are as big as squirrels' ears."

"Don't plant sugar cane until the katydids begin to sing."

"Don't ever keep your chickens near a potato patch. The smell of those potatoes makes hens quit laying and want to brood."

"Red pepper tea cures a bad cold."

"Pine needles, steeped in water overnight, is a good cough remedy when boiled down with sorghum."

And when a farmer knew a tornado was coming, he would race out to his fields and jam a knife in the ground so its blade would cut the winds in half, thus saving his barns and his farmstead.

Times may change.

The farms are larger, managed with computers these days instead of superstition. Mules are no longer used to plow the good earth. New technology has replaced them.

But the legacy of the land is forever.

In Missouri, it is celebrated with Richmond's Mushroom Festival, Forsythe's White Bass Fish Fry, Greenfield's Buffalo Days, Strawberry Festivals at St. James and Bridgeton, East Prairie's Sweet Corn Festival, Crane's Broiler Festival, Eldon's Turkey Festival, Mount Vernon's Berry Festival, and Mexico's Soybean Festival. There are apple festivals and jubilees at Seymour, Peculiar, Waverly, Versailles, Weston, Clarksville and Mount Vernon. Stockton and Alton offer homage to the black walnut. Brunswick has the Pecan Festival. Chili is served up at cookoffs in St. Louis, Cassville, and Washington. Kennett hosts the Show-Me State Championship Barbecue Cookoff. Hermann salutes Cajun food, St. Louis to Polish food. Hermann also has the Great Stone Hill Grape Stomp. And old fashioned ice cream socials take center stage at Versailles and Tuscumbia.

There are community picnics and church suppers, and whenever two or more are gathered together for just about any occasion, their thoughts are on food, and their plates are generally piled high with it.

Tours are even available at Anheuser-Busch and Bardenheier's Wine Cellars, both in St. Louis; Stone Hill Winery in Hermann; Mt. Pleasant Winery in Augusta; Peaceful Bend Vinyard in Steelville; and the St. James, Rosati, and Stoltz Wineries in St. James.

The rich soil of Missouri has been tracked with the footprints of those who have left distinct and distinguished marks on the heritage of America.

When Daniel Boone trekked west toward new frontiers, he found a home in the land that became Missouri. Samuel Clemens ran the muddy banks of the Mississippi River in his hometown of Hannibal long before he traded a steamboat for a writing pen and became Mark Twain. George Caleb Bingham's works of art deftly evoked a placid co-existence of man and his wilderness. Thomas Hart Benton gained recognition as one of America's greatest contemporary artists, but his mural in the State Capitol Building has forever been embroiled in flaming controversy. It featured Frankie and Johnny, the James Boys, Huck Finn and Jim, characters both loved and loathed, instead of characters that had historical impact on the state. And George Washington Carver, the sage of Diamond Grove, unlocked the mystery of the peanut.

Harry Truman had been a Missouri banker, farmer, soldier, county judge and senator. But when he telephoned his 92-year-old mother back in Grandview, after the 1945 inaugural luncheon at the White House, he was calling as Vice President of the United States. Her only words of advice to him were: "Now you behave yourself up there, Harry. You behave yourself."

J. C. Penney named his first place of business the Golden Rule Store, attesting to his belief in the positive mixture of ethics and economics. General Omar Bradley marched away from Missouri to fight and win a world war.

And, in 1925, Charles Lindbergh, a first lieutenant in the Missouri National Guard, was working with a St. Louis aircraft corporation, flying the mail between St. Louis and Chicago. He heard that someone was offering a prize of $25,000 to the first pilot to cross the Atlantic non-stop from New York to Paris. It was a challenge he could not resist nor refuse. Lindbergh raised the necessary capital from a St. Louis businessman and purchased his plane, the Spirit of St. Louis. On May 20, 1927, he soared high above the American coastline, crossed those 3,600 lonely miles of the Atlantic, and landed outside of Paris. His daring flight established the cornerstone of a tradition which became an integral part of Missouri's commercial life, the state's pivotal role in the national aeronautics and aerospace industry.

Agriculture, however, is Missouri's number one industry and largest employer. The harvest and the manufacture of food has long been a key commercial success in the state. Missouri's farmers and ranchers and dairymen have built a strong and a proud reputation in the American marketplace. The food industry within the state lines the shelves of the nation's supermarkets with top brands and the finest quality.

In September 1988, 25 food processors met in St. Louis with the Hawthorn Foundaton to discuss the mutual concerns for the Missouri food industry. From this meeting came the concept for forming the Missouri Food Processors Association to help members produce, process, pack and promote quality foods.

Open to all firms engaged in the processing of food, the association promotes efforts to educate consumers on the benefits of Missouri food items, it sponsors scholarships, and it supports research on food production and processing.

The MPA maintains liaisons with the University of Missouri's educational staff and works with the Missouri Department of Agriculture's AgriMissouri marketing program.

The Agri-Missouri Program, initiated in 1985, is an innovative marketing tool developed to identify Missouri agricultural goods, emphasizing

4

their quality, freshness and availability. It gives consumers within the state an opportunity to recognize and purchase Missouri's own home-grown, home-processed products. As the Department of Agriculture points out, "Given a choice, Missourians will always buy Missouri products."

Throughout the years, Missouri's 4-H Foundation has stood tall, guiding the footsteps of youth whose work, whose efforts have formed a valuable cornerstone of the state.

Missouri 4-H builds leaders in the urban, as well as the rural, crossroads of the state.

It teaches commitment.

And dedication.

And service.

That is a respected tradition.

That is the 4-H legacy.

In Missouri, the work of the farmer, the rancher, the dairyman is never done.

Food manufacturers and processors are actively working every day of the year to help keep the nation, the world fed.

And for decades, 4-H has been educating Missouri youth, preparing them for the job that lies ahead of them.

From generation to generation, the torch is passed, and all become an important, integral part of a never ending season.

Appetizers
&
Snacks

Governor's Favorite Tofu Cheeseball/Dip

1 (10.5-12 oz) pkg tofu
or
8 oz* Mid-America Farms
Onion Dip
½ cup green pepper, chopped
1 tbsp onion, chopped
1 tsp garlic salt
1 pkg dried beef, chopped fine
1-1½ cups pecans, chopped

- Mix all ingredients together and roll in pecans.
- Refrigerate until served.

* For dip – use 12 oz onion dip.

In 1673, Jesuit missionary Jacques Marquette traversed the Wisconsin River with Canadian navigator and tradesman Louis Joliet, who commanded the expedition. Their voyage led them into the "Father of Waters," the mighty Mississippi. Marquette described the most impressive scene of all, the moment when the Mississippi merged with the Missouri:

". . . sailing quietly in clear and calm water, we heard the noise of a rapid, into which we were about to run. I have seen nothing more dreadful. And accumulation of large and entire trees, branches, and floating islands, were issing from the mouth of the River *Pekitanoui*, with such impetuosity that we could not without great danger risk passing through it."

But pass through it they did. This voyage proved the Mississippi was not a route to the Pacific as was desperately hoped for by the early explorers. The French would call the river *Missouri* after the Indian village located nearby.

Cheese Nut Rolls

1 lb Morningland Dairy Natural Sharp Cheddar Cheese, grated
2 cups flour, sifted
dash chili powder
salt to taste
¼ lb butter
2 cups Miller Farms Pecans, finely chopped

- Put cheese in bowl; sprinkle with flour, chili powder, and salt.
- Cut in butter.
- Knead to smooth dough.
- Roll on lightly floured board to a rectangle ¼" thick.
- Sprinkle evenly with pecans, press lightly into dough.
- Roll as you would a jelly roll.
- Wrap in wax paper and chill until firm.
- Cut into crosswise slices ⅓" thick.
- Place on cookie sheet, bake at 375 degrees until golden brown, about 12 minutes. Serve immediately.
- Makes about 2 dozen.

The Otoe-Missouri Indians, according to legend, migrated southwest from native grounds in the Great Lakes region in search of buffalo. A dispute between two chieftains led to a schism which resulted in the creation of two distinct and separate tribes, the Otoe and the Missouri. By 1833, the Missouri tribe had all but disappeared from the land which bears its name. Its people were moved south to a reservation in Oklahoma, and the Bureau of Indian Affairs lists no Missouri Indians living in Missouri today.

Cheese Ball

1 (8 oz) pkg Philadelphia Brand® Cream Cheese
1 cup sharp cheese, grated
1 tsp Aunt Joan's Ozark Country Mustard
6 drops hot pepper sauce
paprika, if desired this gives a yellow color
1 tbsp chopped pimento
¼ teaspoon salt
1 tsp Worcestershire

- Soften cream cheese in a bowl over warm water.
- Add remaining ingredients and blend well.
- Chill in refrigerator before shaping.
- Yield: About 1 lb.

Sausage and Rice Balls

3 cups biscuit mix
1 lb Corn King Sausage
8 oz Morningland Dairy Cheese, grated
2 cups Della Gourmet Rice, cooked

- Mix biscuit mix, sausage and cheese well.
- Fold in rice.
- Form into small balls and bake at 350 degrees on a cooking sheet until brown.
- Makes 25-30 balls.

Best Ever Heavenly Hot Dip

2 pkg Heavenly Hot Lentils Divine
¾ cup mayonnaise
2 limes
1 tsp salt
1 pkg flour tortillas, toasted

- Boil lentils in 3½ cups of water until very tender, 40-45 minutes.
- Combine cooled lentils; mayonnaise, juice of the limes, and salt in a blender and blend until very creamy. Chill.
- Serve chilled with toasted tortillas. Also, delicious with crackers, vegetables or rye bread.

To toast tortillas:
- Cut each tortilla into 8 wedges.
- Place on cookie sheet.
- Bake at 350 degrees for 10-15 minutes or until crispy.
- Use as dippers.

Classic Nacho Dip

½ cup chopped onion
2 tbsp margarine
1 lb process cheese spread, cubed
1 (8 oz) jar Old El Paso Thick 'n Chunky Salsa
2 tbsp cilantro, chopped

- Saute onions in margarine; reduce heat to low.
- Add remaining ingredients; stir until process cheese spread is melted.
- Serve hot with tortilla chips or vegetable dippers, if desired. Yields: 3 cups.

Microwave:
- Microwave onions and margarine in 1½-qt bowl on HIGH 1½ minutes or until tender.
- Add remaining ingredients; mix well. Microwave 5 minutes or until thoroughly heated, stirring after 3 minutes.

Iron County, with its rich, historical past, was the birthplace of Missouri 4-H. Ulysses S. Grant had received the commission of Brigadier General from President Lincoln in the county seat of Ironton in 1861. Old Pilot Knob provided the natural terrain and protection for the Union Army against a charging Confederate brigade.

Creamy Horseradish Dipper

½ lb process cheese spread, grated
½ cup Sauce-Works Horseradish Sauce
⅓ cup milk
2 doz chicken nuggets, hot and cooked

Microwave:

- Combine process cheese spread, horseradish sauce and milk in saucepan over low heat until smooth.
- Serve with hot cooked chicken nuggets.
- Makes 1⅓ cups.
- Microwave process cheese spread, horseradish sauce and milk in 1 qt bowl on High 4-5 minutes or until process cheese spread is melted, stirring every 2 minutes. Serve as directed.

Shrimp Au Vin Dipper

½ lb process cheese spread, cubed
2 tbsp dry white wine
½ tsp dried basil leaves, crushed
1 (4¼ oz) can tiny shrimp, drained and minced

- Stir process cheese spread, wine and basil over low heat until smooth.
- Stir in shrimp; heat thoroughly, stirring occasionally.
- Serve with assorted vegetable dippers or bread sticks.
- Makes 2½ cups.

Spicy Fiesta Nachos

1 bag La Casita's Homestyle
Tortilla Chips
1 can La Casita's Deluxe Nacho
Cheese Dip
1 (16 oz) can refried beans
1 (16 oz) jar La Casita's
Homestyle Picante Salsa,
(Mild, Hot or Thick 'n Chunky)
1 small container Hiland
Sour Cream
2 green onions, chopped
1 cup Cheddar cheese, grated
1 small can black olives, sliced
1 small jar jalapeno peppers,
sliced (optional)

- Select 2 doz flat triangular tortilla chips from the bag and arrange on platter.
- Heat refried beans and mix with cheese dip. Keep warm. Spread bean/cheese mixture on chips.
- Add a small amount of picante on each chip, and top with a small dab of sour cream.
- Sprinkle cheese, green onions, and crown with a sliced black olive and sliced jalapeno, (optional).
- Serves 3-4.

Jan's European Herb Cheese

1 (8 oz) pkg cream cheese,
softened
¼ cup butter, unsalted, softened
1 pkt Jan's European
Herb Cheese

- Mix all ingredients together and chill.
- Serve with fresh crudites, bagel chips or crackers.

In 1914, B. P. Burnham organized the first corn clubs in the old school on Knob Street in Ironton and then in the small community of Annapolis.

Built on ideas Burnham received from R. H. Emberson, the State Club Leader from 1914 to 1923, teachers and leaders worked with young men to teach them how to grow corn. The clubs' members were required to grow one acre of corn, applying bone meal and barnyard manure, and measuring the yields.

These successful corn clubs were the embryos from which 4-H was born, patterning 4-H Club Work after Burnham's work in Iron County.

Aunt Nene's Good-For-You Dip

2 cups Central Dairy Cottage Cheese
2 tbsp juice from Aunt Nene's Savory Okra
¼ cup scallions or mild onions, chopped
2 tbsp parsley
salt to taste
freshly ground pepper to taste
6-8 fresh basil leaves

- For the proper creamy texture, you must use a blender or food processor.
- Puree all the ingredients in a blender or food processor, and chill.
- Tastes garden-fresh with raw vegetables or Country Cooked Potato Chips.
- Makes about 2 cups.

Missouri 4-H has no bigger supporter than Jeannine Williams, originator of Aunt Nene's Specialty Foods in Lucerne. Jeannine said, "As a 4-H member, I learned so many things, both tangible and intangible. I learned various life-skills, how-to-skills, self-confidence and numerous leadership skills.

"Through 4-H, I also learned life-attitudes. One such attitude, instilled by both my parents and 4-H, was what I like to call "lattice works." It's now a part of my business philosophy.

" 'Lattice works' is a simple belief and understanding that everybody depends on everybody else, whether it's in 4-H, business or life — just like a piece of lattice-work, each part linked and dependent upon each other."

Jeannine's "lattice works" philosophy has been the cornerstone for building Aunt Nene's Specialty Foods. A family-owned business nestled in northern Missouri's cattle country, the business began as a result of the farm crisis nine years ago. As a way to generate extra income, Jeannine Williams began sharing the unique tastes of her treasured farm-family recipes.

From zesty sweet dill slices to fruited zucchini marmalade, Jeannine's flavorful delicacies are meticulously hand-packed and processed in small batches. Using only the freshest ingredients, strict standards ensure authentic home-made taste in every jar. Jeannine, her husband, Gordan, and their two sons, Chad and Codie, grow much of their own produce in their organic gardens. Her products have no preservatives, MSG or artificial flavors, and are made from all natural ingredients.

The 'Nene' in Aunt Nene is a family nickname given to Jeannine by her four brothers, and is now repeated by several nephews and nieces. The young relatives each have their favorite product, and often ask, "Is this Aunt Nene's?" before taking a bite of pickles, jams or jellies.

Fern Valentine, Jeannine's mother, personally sews all of the fancy jar "toppers" for the condiments. Loring and Mark Pickering, Jeannine's aunt and uncle, handcraft the wooden crates used to create lovely gift packages. Gordan's parents, Junior and Jean Williams, lend their services to the business in countless ways.

The whole family works together — sisters-in-law and other relatives, plus friends and nearby neighbors. Each believe in and contribute to the success of Aunt Nene's Specialty Foods. This success is evidenced by the fact that this small Missouri business now markets internationally, as well as nationwide.

Aunt Nene's Easy Deviled Ham Spread

2 (4½ oz) cans Underwood's
Deviled Ham
1 tbsp pimento, minced
1 tbsp juice from Aunt Nene's
Cracklin'-Crisp Bread and
Butter Pickles
1 tbsp onion, minced
½ cup mayonnaise
½ cup celery, minced

- Mix all ingredients, chill.
- Serve with a variety of interesting crackers, chips, or on a variety of breads.

The land that became Missouri was a cornerstone of the Louisiana Purchase. During those early years when the West was a distant frontier, Missouri was first claimed for France by LaSalle in 1682, and the French, who built the first permanent settlement of Ste. Genevieve, left a definite and distinct impact on the country's culture.

Spain took control of the Missouri lands in 1762, jealously holding onto them for the next 40 years, finally ceding the territory back to France.

For Napoleon Bonaparte, the frontier was simply too rugged, too troublesome, too far away from the homeland to rule, so he sold the huge French holdings to the United States for $15 million.

It just may have been the greatest real estate bargain of them all.

Missouri was organized as a territory in 1812 and admitted to the Union as the nation's twenty-fourth state on August 10, 1821.

Bacon and Vegetable Pizza

1 (12 oz) pkg Farmland Bacon
2 (8 oz) pkgs refrigerated crescent dinner rolls
¾ cup plain lowfat yogurt
¾ cup mayonnaise
2 tsp sugar
2 tsp Fines Herbs
1 tsp dillweed
dash garlic powder
4 green onions with tops, thinly sliced
1 medium carrot, shredded
⅔ cup broccoli, finely chopped
1 (4 oz) cup Mid-America Farms Part-Skim Mozzarella Cheese, shredded

- Cook bacon until browned and crisp; cool and crumble.
- To make crust, unroll dinner rolls and pat into a 17"x11"x1" baking sheet.
- Bake at 375 degrees for 11 minutes or until lightly browned; cool.
- In a small bowl, combine yogurt, mayonaise, sugar, herbs, dillweed and garlic powder; spread over crust.
- Sprinkle on onions, carrot, broccoli, cheese and bacon. Cover with aluminum foil or plastic wrap. Press gently to "set" toppings.
- Refrigerate until serving time. (May be held in refrigerator 1-2 days.).
- Makes 32 appetizer-size servings.

Cocktail Pizza

1 pizza crust, baked
1 recipe Jan's European
Herb Cheese (see page 12)
1 cup fresh vegetables, finely
chopped, (choose from a
combination of broccoli,
cauliflower, shredded carrot, red
or green pepper, red onion)

- Spread herb cheese on baked pizza crust.
- Arrange vegetables on top of herb cheese.
- Cut in slices and serve.

Hors d'oeuvres Snacks

melba toast
Aunt Joan's Ozark
Country Mustard

- For great hors d'oeuvres make some fresh thin melba toast.
- Spread or dip mustard on the toast for a simple, fast delicious snack.

Antipasto all'Italiano   *Italy's Antipasto*

1 small can Italian tuna fish
4-6 oz Volpi Genova Salame,
sliced thin
4-6 oz Volpi Prosciutto,
sliced thin
4-6 oz Volpi Coppa (hot or
sweet), sliced thin
4-6 oz Volpi Sopressata (hot or
sweet), sliced thin
4 anchovy filets
2 celery hearts, cut in halves
lengthwise
8 large green olives
2 tsp capers
4 artichoke hearts in oil
1 small can pimentos

4 tomato slices
4 vinegar peppers
8 black ripe olives

- Use a large oval platter.
- Place tuna fish and imported antipasto in center of dish and arrange all the other ingredients around, making as pretty a pattern as you can.
- Serve with crusty Italian bread and butter.
- Serves 4.

17

Mary Beth Gentry brought more than 10 years experience in the food industry to the founding of Flavors of the Heartland in 1988. Designed as a company to help small family-owned companies in Missouri to market their food products, Flavors of the Heartland started with 10 boutique companies which had annual gross revenues of $20,000 to $1 million.

Outstanding food products, ranging from mustards and salsa to gourmet rice, popcorn and sausages, Flavors of the Heartland works with the company to decide on packaging, promotional materials, distribution networks and other marketing elements. Heartland's clients' products are placed in supermarkets and specialty stores, and are promoted at wholesale and retail trade shows.

Flavors of the Heartland is representative of the Missouri enterpreneurial spirit that promotes the development of distinctive, quality products, and enhances the economic well being of small, independent businesses.

Salmon Pate

2 pkts Jan's Salmon Pate Seasoning Mix
2 tbsp water
1 (7½ oz) can salmon, drained
1 (3 oz) pkg cream cheese, softened

- Place all ingredients in food processor or mixer bowl and mix until smooth.
- Chill.
- Yields: 2 cups.

Canapes:
- Place pate mixture in pastry bag and pipe mixture into miniature cream puffs, hollowed out cherry tomatoes, or snow peas.
- Using a rosette tip, pipe onto bread or cucumber slices.
- Garnish with sprig of dill or capers.

To Mold:
- Line a 2 cup decorative fish mold with plastic wrap. Fill with salmon mixture. Chill several hours or overnight.
- To unmold, invert mold on serving platter and remove plastic wrap. Garnish with lemon slices and fresh dill.
- Serve with crackers or cocktail size rye bread.

Smoky Links in Pastry

1 (8 oz) pkg crescent rolls, refrigerated
16 Seitz Smoky Links
2 cans pineapple tidbits, drained
½ cup Missouri Classic Barbecue Sauce

- Open rolls, unroll dough and separate into triangles. Cut each triangle into halves lengthwise.
- Slit Seitz Smoky Links lengthwise, but not all the way through.
- Stuff 2-3 pineapple tidbits into each Smoky Link.
- Spoon about 1 tsp sauce into the slit.
- Put 1 filled smoky on the wide end of the dough and roll up as directed on the package. Put point side down on greased cookie sheet.
- Bake in a pre-heated 400 degree oven for 10 minutes or until golden brown.
- Remove from sheet with a pancake turner and serve immediately while hot.
- Makes 16 hors d'oeuvres.

Missouri 4-H roots were planted in 1914, when agriculture came of age and the Smith-Lever Act gave birth to the Cooperative Extension Service. Seventy-six years ago Missouri girls and boys, in primarily rural areas, were enrolled in the State Extension youth program known as Boys and Girls Club Work. It wasn't until 1927 that the name was changed to 4-H Club Work. Since that time 4-H has reached from the farm into the towns and cities to enrich the lives of a million young Missourians.

Prosciutto, Melon and Kiwi Hors D'oeuvres

2 ripe cantaloupe melons
24 Volpi Prosciutto slices, thin
6 ripe kiwis, peeled and thinly sliced
2 limes, cut into wedges, (optional garnish)

- Make 36 large melon balls from the melon.
- Arrange equal portions of the melon balls, Volpi Prosciutto and kiwi slices decoratively on 6 individual plates. Garnish if desired.
- Serves 6.

Big Batch Basic Granola Mix

12 cups old-fashioned oats
7 cups wheat germ
1 cup sunflower or
pumpkin seeds
1 cup Byrd's Pecans,
chopped or broken
1 tbsp salt
2 cups soybean oil
3 tbsp vanilla
1½ cups Barker's Honey
2 cups dried fruit, (raisins,
apricots, dates, figs, peaches or
cherries)

- Mix together first 5 ingredients in a large bowl.
- Mix together oil, vanilla and honey. Add to oat mixture.
- Thoroughly mix everything except the dried fruit.
- Spread in thin layers on shallow baking pans.
- Toast in 300 degree oven 30-45 minutes, or until golden brown. Stir often to prevent scorching around the edges.
- When thoroughly cooled, mix in dried fruit and store in airtight containers.
- Makes about 24 cups.

Curried Popcorn Mix

2 tbsp plus 2 tsp soybean
oil margarine
1 tsp Worcestershire sauce
½ tsp curry powder
⅛ tsp garlic powder
2 cups crispy corn cereal
¼ cup Fancy Farms Popcorn,
(4 cups popped)
½ cup dried apricots, chopped
⅓ cup raisins
3 tbsp coconut, flaked

- Melt margarine in a non-stick skillet, remove from heat.
- Add Worcestershire sauce, curry powder and garlic powder, stir well.
- Add cereal, stir to coat.
- Combine remaining ingredients in a large bowl.
- Add cereal mixture, toss gently.
- Yield 7 cups.

Missouri has long been the home of an independent breed of people. And their slogan is "Show-me."

No one really knows how long the expression has been around, but it gained fame in 1899 when Congressman Willard D. Vandiver of Cape Girardeau County said in a Philadelphia speech:

"I'm from Missouri; you've got to show me."

His words typified the attitude of Missouri, which, from that moment on, became the "Show-Me State."

Over the Coals Spiced Popcorn

½ cup Fancy Farms Popcorn, unpopped
Kingsford® Briquets
2 tbsp butter or margarine
½ tsp Worcestershire sauce
½ tsp chili powder
½ tsp lemon pepper
¼ tsp garlic powder
¼ tsp onion powder
⅛ tsp salt

- Pop popcorn over briquets in long handled fireplace corn popper. Hold directly over, but not touching hot Kingsford® Briquets.
- Shake vigorously until corn is popped, about 3-4 minutes.
- In saucepan, combine all ingredients but popcorn. Set on edge of grill to melt butter.
- Toss butter mixture with popped popcorn.

Diversity is the key word when it comes to discussing agriculture in Missouri. Production of hay, rice, soybeans, wheat, corn, cotton, sorghum, black walnuts, tobacco, barley, fruit, and fescue, to name a few crops, defines the abundance found here. Once there was even a colony of horseradish growers in St. Louis County.

The cattle industry is second only to Texas for its beef cow production.

Soft drink pioneer Vess Jones created a new carbonated beverage called Whistle Orange in 1916. The new drink was an immediate success, and a springboard for Vess Beverages, Inc. At one time, Whistle Orange was bottled by more than 400 soft drink bottlers around the country. Jones began producing other flavors which became known as Vess soda.

Then came the disastrous stock market crash of 1929. Vess Jones sold his company to Leroy Schneeberger for $10,000. Schneeberger proved to be one of the early soft drink industry's most imaginative marketers, and under his direction the company prospered.

Vess became a leading brand in many parts of the country and was always at the forefront of change and innovation. Vess was the first bottler in the United States to offer instant cash awards by printing prize amounts on the inside of bottle caps. And Vess was decades ahead of the competition by introducing the first caffeine-free cola in 1946. Continuing to progress, Vess introduced the first 16-ounce returnable bottle to St. Louis with the 3V Cola, the 3V standing for vim, vigor and vitality.

Unfortunately, the glory and growth came to an abrupt end. In 1968, Schneeberger sold the company to an out-of-town conglomerate, and sales took a downward spiral. By 1975, Vess sales had declined to 650,000 cases annually.

Then young Don Schneeberger, who had worked for many years at Vess with his father, Leroy, purchased the ailing company and began the rebuilding process.

Under the younger Schneeberger's leadership, Vess has once again become one of the largest independent soft drink manufacturers in the U.S. Company sales have surpassed the 11 million case mark, and continue to grow at a rapid pace.

The privately-held, St. Louis-based corporation now sells Vess sodas in 33 states and numerous foreign countries. With modern production facilities and state-of-the-art equipment, Vess produces more total cases than any other soft drink bottler in St. Louis. In addition, Vess soft drinks are produced by a franchise bottler in Omaha, Nebraska, and by contract packers in other cities.

In 1988, a highly sophisticated reverse osmosis water purification system was installed in the St. Louis plant. Unlike other bottlers who use chemically treated water, Vess uses only purified water, and removes all salt from its products. No other soft drink manufacturer in the country offers the consumer both of these qualities.

The new purification system has led to the introduction of Vess Bottled Waters which are totally free of salt, sodium, sugar, calories and pollutants.

Vess began bottling 100% NutraSweet Diet Vess flavors in 1989. The use of NutraSweet brand sweetener is another testimony of Vess' dedication to superior products.

With sales of Vess beverages topping six and one half million cases in St. Louis alone in 1989, Vess continues to grow in the Missouri market, being third behind only Pepsi and Coca-Cola.

Vess Jones would be proud if he could see Vess Beverages today, strong and committed to the tradition of excellence he started so long ago.

Watermelon Popsicles

½ Missouri Watermelon
2 tsp fresh lemon juice
½ cup sugar
½ cup Vess Distilled Water

- Cut watermelon into cubes and rub through a strainer to remove seeds, making 3 cups watermelon juice.
- In small saucepan mix together sugar and water, simmer 3 minutes.
- Remove from heat, stir in watermelon juice and lemon juice. Turn into 2 ice trays.
- Freeze until very mushy and insert a popsicle stick in each cube. Freeze.
- Makes about 36 small popsicles.

Soups
&
Salads

Creamy Broccoli Soup

¼ cup onion, chopped
1 tbsp margarine
2 cups milk
1 (8 oz) pkg Philadelphia Brand®
Cream Cheese, cubed
¾ lb process cheese spread, cubed
⅛ tsp ground nutmeg
dash of pepper

- Saute onions in butter in 2-qt saucepan, until tender.
- Add milk and cream cheese; stir over medium heat until cream cheese is melted.
- Add remaining ingredients; heat thoroughly stirring occasionally.
- Serves 4-5.

Cream of Zucchini Soup

4 medium zucchini
2 cups water
dash of salt
2 tbsp fresh parsley, chopped
2 (4 oz) cans Old El Paso Green Chilies, chopped
2 tbsp butter
2 tbsp onion, finely chopped
1 tbsp flour
1 (12 oz) can Pet Evaporated Milk
1 cup chicken broth
parsley leaves for garnish

- Wash zucchini. Cut off stem ends, then cut in large pieces.
- Place in saucepan with water and salt.
- Bring to a boil.
- Cover, cook 20 minutes.
- Remove zucchini, let cool.
- Place zucchini, 1 cup cooking liquid, parsley and chilies in blender; blend until pureed.
- Saute onion in melted butter.
- Stir in flour. Cook and stir one minute.
- Add pureed mixture, milk and broth. Stir to blend.
- Season with salt if needed.
- Stir over medium heat for 10-15 minutes, just below boiling.
- Serve at once or chill and serve cold.
- Garnish with parsley.
- Makes 6 servings.

Pet Incorporated of St. Louis gained prominence after the Spanish-American War when soldiers and sailors came home and told about the "tin cow" milk that stayed fresh after days, weeks and even months in the field. The "tin cow" that appeared on an early label still appears today on cans of Pet Evaporated Milk.

Founded as the Helvetia Milk Condensing Company in 1885 in Highland, Illinois, the little company dreamed of developing a clean, fresh milk that would keep indefinitely on the pantry of every American home. In those pre-refrigeration days, milk was transported by horse-drawn wagons over bumpy dirt roads, arriving at its destination in less than perfect condition.

After many years of experimentation, a group led by a man named Louis Latzer was successful in canning unsweetened milk.

The evaporated milk was sold under several brand names, but the one that was the most popular was "Our Pet," introduced around the turn of the century in a baby-sized can that sold for five cents. It became so popular that in 1923 the Helvetia Milk Condensing Company adopted the name Pet Milk Company.

After moving the headquarters to St. Louis in the 1920s, dozens of milk condensaries were built throughout the East, the Midwest and the South. When no ready sources of milk were found, Pet helped local farmers develop dairy stock and pastures. When the new dairy farmers produced an overabundance of fresh milk, Pet found other uses for it. Starting with ice cream, Pet built a fresh daily business that is still healthy and thriving today.

Pet Incorporated has always been a partner in the community. When Pet Evaporated Milk was a popular infant food, the company did its part to help bewildered parents of triplets and quadruplets cope with their sudden population explosion. Beginning with the tiny Kasper quads born in 1926 in Passaic, New Jersey, Pet "adopted" 10 sets of quads, setting up trust funds to pay for clothing, housing and medical care. In addition, more than 1,400 sets of triplets were provided with a constant supply of Pet Milk.

After World War II, most Americans began to enjoy a higher standard of living. Refrigerators could be found in almost every home, and prepared formulas began to replace evaporated milk for infant feeding. Pet knew it had to change its business in order to survive. In 1955, the company took its first step in a new direction when it purchased the Pet-Ritz frozen pie business.

Over the years Pet acquired other well-known brand names: Progresso, Old El Paso and Underwood, famous for the "Red Devil" ham. Pet introduced Heartland cereal, and coined the term "natural cereal." Altogether, Pet manufactures hundreds of different products under dozens of brands including Whitman's "Sampler" chocolates, Aunt Fanny's Bakery pecan twirls, Accent flavor enhancer, B&M baked beans and brown bread, Pet-Ritz pies, Downyflake, Hollywood, Las Palmas and Van de Kamp's.

French Onion Soup

6 tbsp Mid-America Farms Butter
2 cups onion, thinly sliced
2 tsp flour
1 tbsp sugar
1 tsp dry mustard
1 (10¾ oz) can chicken broth
1 (10¾ oz) can beef broth
¼ cup Stone Hill Vidal Wine
2 tsp Worcestershire sauce
1 cup croutons
¼ cup Parmesan cheese
1 cup Mid-America Farms
Mozzarella Cheese, shredded

- Place butter in deep 3 qt casserole. Microwave at full power 1½ minutes, or until melted.
- Stir in onions.
- Microwave at full power 25-30 minutes or until onions are browned and carmelized, stirring every 5 minutes.
- Stir in flour, sugar and mustard; mix well.
- Stir in broth, wine and Worcestershire sauce.
- Microwave at full power for 9-10 minutes or until mixture thickens slightly and bubbles, stirring 4 times.
- Ladle into 4 soup bowls and top each serving with croutons.
- Sprinkle on cheeses and microwave at full power for 2-2½ minutes, or until cheese melts, rearranging bowls once.

Early Missouri was ruled by the French Catholics who settled the land.

Their religion was their government.

As a result, the first Protestant sermon ever heard in Missouri was delivered by a minister named John Clark who stood on a rock in the Mississippi River and yelled to the few who gathered on the muddy banks to hear his words.

He preached until his throat went dry, he lost his voice, and the crowd melted away.

But he wasn't allowed to preach on Missouri soil at all. It was against the law.

The beauty and ruggedness of Iron County produced a special breed of men and women. One of these men was B. P. Burnham, Iron County's first superintendent of schools. A towering man, six-feet, two inches tall and weighing more than 200 pounds, Burnham's dark hair and blue eyes accented his classical features. Gentle by nature, he could be quite forceful when the occasion demanded it, especially during his years as Iron County Treasurer.

A man who owned a great deal of property came into Burnham's office to pay his taxes. When the taxes were more than he thought they should be, the man refused to pay. Walking across the room and picking up the man's expensive overcoat which he had laid on a nearby chair, Burnham replied emphatically "No taxes, no overcoat."

The man quickly paid his taxes.

Hillbilly Bean Soup

1½ cups Hillbilly
Bean Soup Mix
1 tbsp salt and pepper to taste
1 lb Farmland Ham,
cut in pieces
1 clove garlic
1 large (16 oz) can tomatoes
1 large onion, chopped
1 lemon, juice of
1 pod green or red pepper,
chopped

• Wash bean mixture.
• Cover with water. Add salt and pepper and soak for 3 hours or overnight.
• Drain water and put beans in 2 quarts of fresh water.
• Add remaining ingredients.
• Cook all day (at least 4 hours).
• Serve hot.
• May be kept in covered container in refrigerator up to 4 days.

Chicken, Corn and Corned Beef Chowder

½ cup salt pork, diced
1 medium onion, chopped
½ cup celery, chopped
¼ cup green pepper, chopped
2 cups chicken broth
1 medium potato
½ bay leaf
¼ tsp paprika
½ tsp salt
3 tbsp flour
½ cup milk
1 cup whole kernel corn
2 cups Hudson Chicken,
cooked and diced
2 cups Boyle's Corned Beef,
cooked and diced
1½ cup half and half
parsley, chopped

- Brown salt pork in skillet. Remove pork and reserve.
- Saute onion, celery and green pepper in the drippings.
- Add chicken broth, potato, bay leaf, paprika and salt. Simmer until potato is tender.
- Blend flour with milk. Add to soup.
- Boil 1 minute; add corn, chicken, corned beef, diced pork and half and half.
- Heat to serving temperature.
- Garnish with parsley.
- Serves 8.

Chili-Corn Chowder

1 tbsp soybean oil margarine
1 cup onion, chopped
½ cup green pepper, chopped
2 tbsp unpeeled lemon, chopped
1 bay leaf
2 tbsp flour
1 tsp chicken bouillon granules
¼ tsp chili powder
⅛ tsp pepper
1 cup water
1 (13 oz) can Pet Light
Evaporated Skimmed Milk
1 (12 oz) can whole kernel corn
2 tomatoes, peeled, seeded
and chopped
2 tsp green chiles, chopped
1 tbsp fresh parsley, chopped

- In a large saucepan, melt margarine.
- Add onion, green pepper, lemon and bay leaf. Saute until just tender.
- Blend in flour, bouillon granules, chili powder and pepper.
- Add water and milk; cook over medium heat, stirring constantly, until thickened.
- Stir in corn, tomatoes and green chiles. Reduce heat and simmer 1 miuute.
- Remove bay leaf and stir in parsley.
- Serves 4-6.

Joseph Murphy stood in the dirt streets of St. Louis and looked West.

He was a wagon maker.

And he knew that men and women both considered the far frontier as a land of promise.

He could help get them there.

So he fashioned huge covered wagons with seven-foot wheels, and he believed:

"Dreams are only frustration on the hoof if you don't have the mechanical means to make them come true."

His wagons gave those dreams a chance to succeed in a land where only the hardy and the stubborn survived.

Burger's Ozark Country Ham Hocks

- Wash ham hocks with lukewarm water.
- Parboil hock for approximately 10 minutes.
- Hock is now ready to use as desired.
- If you like a milder tasting ham hock boil longer.

Split Pea Soup

1 lb (2¼ cups) green split peas
1½ cups onion, sliced
1 tsp salt
½ tsp pepper
1 cup celery, diced
1 cup carrots, diced
Burger's Ozark Country Ham Hocks
salt to taste

- Cover peas with 2 qts cold water and soak overnight.
- Simmer gently 2 minutes then soak 1 hour.
- Add ham hock, onion and seasoning.
- Bring to boiling; cover, reduce heat, and simmer (don't boil) 1½ hrs.
- Stir occasionally, remove hock; cut off meat and dice.
- Return meat to soup; add vegetables.
- Cook slowly, uncovered, 30-40 minutes. Salt to taste.
- Serves 6-8.

Watermelon Rind Preserves

6 cups Missouri Watermelon Rind, diced
3 oranges
2 lemons
4½ cups sugar

- Peel the green skin off the outside of the rind of watermelon and cut out the red meat.
- Slice the rind into cubes that are about 1″ square.
- Seed the oranges and lemons and cut them into thin slices.
- Add the fruit slices and sugar to the cubed rind.
- Boil slowly until the rind is clear. This should take about 2 hours.
- Add color as you desire before filling jars.
- Fill sterile jars and process following recommended method.

Hornersville, near the Arkansas border, is the watermelon capitol of Missouri. In 1985, a 210-pound watermelon was grown there, selling at auction for $1,500.

Hot Grilled Apple Salad

2 cups Missouri Apples, cored and thinly sliced
3 cups red cabbage, shredded
4 tsp butter or margarine, cut up
3 tbsp red wine vinegar
4 tsp sugar
¾ tsp salt
¼ tsp caraway seed
¼ tsp pepper

- In bowl, toss all ingredients. Turn out onto 18″x24″ piece of heavy-duty foil.
- Fold edges around apple mixture; seal edges tightly.
- Grill packet, on covered grill, over medium-hot Kingsford® Briquets 45 minutes or until apples are tender, turning packet every 15 minutes.

Missouri 4-H develops winning attitudes among its members. As far back as 1933, Roy Lentz of Independence, wrote, "Probably one of the hardest tasks in life is learning how to win without feeling superior to those who lost and to lose without feeling the judge was unfair.

"We, as club members, have learned to congratulate the winner instead of complaining if defeated. This attitude is hard at first, but over several years' training, it becomes a part of one's character. In the words of his Club's motto, 'learn to win without bragging and to lose without squealing.'"

Mixed Fruit Compote

3 cups Missouri Blueberries
1 cup raspberries
1 cup blackberries
1 cup strawberries
¼ cup orange juice
sugar or sweetener to taste
1 banana

- Mix fruit and juice – except banana.
- Add sugar or sweetener to taste; allow to stand at least 2 hours.
- Add banana when ready to serve.
- This fruit is great alone or on ice-cream or with your favorite shortcake.

Artichoke Hearts and Pecans

2 (#2) cans artichoke hearts, drained
2 tbsp butter
2 tbsp flour
1 cup Hiland Cream
salt and pepper, to taste
hot pepper sauce, to taste
½ cup Midwestern Pecan Co. Pecans, broken
¼ cup bread crumbs
2 tbsp Progresso Parmesan Cheese

- Arrange artichoke hearts in small casserole.
- Blend butter and flour in saucepan; add cream.
- Cook, stirring constantly, until thickened. Season with salt, pepper, and hot pepper sauce.
- Pour sauce over artichoke hearts; add pecans. Sprinkle with bread crumbs and cheese.
- Bake at 300 degrees until bubbly.

Adventurers came forth to settle in Upper Louisiana shortly after the Americans won their independence from Great Britain. Among those seeking land and opportunity was a Kentuckian named Daniel Boone. He moved his family, became a prominent citizen, farmed, and manufactured salt in his new home. Boone settled down near the Femme Osage Creek, not far from St. Louis. A salt lick trail from St. Louis to Howard County was known as the "Booneslick Trail."

Bacon Lettuce and Tomato Salad

For a summer treat try:
3 ripe tomatoes
½ medium head lettuce
1 cup croutons
8 slices Alewel's Sugar Cured Bacon, crisp cooked and coarsely crumbled
½ cup mayonnaise or salad dressing
salt and pepper

- Cut tomatoes in wedges.
- Add with remaining ingredients.
- Toss lightly.
- Season with salt and pepper.
- Serves 4-5.

Missouri Salad

1 large head romaine lettuce
3 navel oranges, peeled and sliced
2 avocadoes, peeled and sliced
1 red onion, thinly sliced
1 cucumber, thinly sliced
1 cup Ott's Creamy Buttermilk Dressing
½ cup toasted almonds, sliced

- Tear lettuce into large salad bowl.
- Peel and slice oranges.
- Peel and slice avocadoes; toss in the orange juice to prevent browning. Drain.
- Combine lettuce, oranges, avocado, red onion, cucumber and toss lightly with Ott's Creamy Buttermilk Dressing.
- Sprinkle with toasted sliced almonds.

More than four decades ago, Walter Ott, a Carthage, Missouri, petroleum engineer, realized his dream of going into the restaurant business, and in the process founded a company that has become a premier Missouri institution, Ott Food Products.

Walter wanted to serve a salad dressing like his mother used to make, but didn't have the recipe. Armed with his chemistry know-how, his innate perfectionism, and his neighbors' taste buds, he finally succeeded in matching his mother's blend and began serving it on the cafe's salads. Diners loved the dressing and started asking if they could take some home.

The businessman in Walter was quick to fulfill these requests, with the help of his wife, Ruby, and his only employee, Allene Wilson. They mixed three-gallon batches of the original recipe, poured the mixture into eight-ounce bottles, and glued on labels. Ott's Famous Salad Dressing was born, and at 25 cents a bottle, it was a bargain, even in the 1940s.

Travelers through Carthage from across the country were attracted to the cafe by "word-of-mouth" descriptions of the flavorful dressing. Celebrities like Clark Gable and Gene Autry went out of their way to stop by the restaurant and buy bottles "to go." People sent letters from across the country and all over the world requesting the dressing—some by the case. So many bottles were requested that Walter Ott closed the restaurant in 1948 and began to concentrate solely on the salad dressing business.

The little company received its first 25-case order from Aurora Grocery, and the orders kept coming in. Most of the cases of Ott's Famous Dressing were sent off on common carrier trucks, but Walter personally made the runs to Webb City and Joplin in his old Plymouth.

Walter decided to develop a barbecue sauce as unique in flavor as his salad dressing. He began by tasting other sauces on the market, using his knack for distinguishing individual ingredients by taste. Again his chemistry background helped him, causing him to wear out three slide rules figuring the secret proportions that went into his sauce. Neighbors, employees and kids were the "guinea pigs" for tasting the sauce. Walter thought kids gave the most honest opinions, and if kids liked the sauce, it was good. Finally, through trial and error and extensive taste-testing, Ott's Plantation Barbecue Sauce was created.

Wanting to further add to his product line, he set about to create another distinctive salad dressing, this time with an Italian flavor. Unfortunately, he died in 1966 before completing it.

Ott's Italian and Ott's Ozark Maid Buttermilk Dressing were concocted by new owners, Roy Moore and Jack Crede, with the same slide-rule precision of the founder. The two CPA's purchased the company in 1979 from Walter's widow, Ruby.

Jack and Roy keep the development-ball rolling, with an eye to low-calorie, low sodium recipes using all natural ingredients. The salad dressing innovators from Carthage continue the legacy of Walter Ott and his commitment to keeping the recipe simple, yet perfect, by integrating scientific know-how into each formula.

As Roy and Jack explain, "Walter wouldn't have it any other way."

We Like It A L'Ott's

2 qts fresh spinach and lettuce
2 hard-cooked eggs, sliced
¼ lb Farmland Bacon, fried crisp and crumbled
croutons, to taste
green onions with tops, chopped, to taste
Ott's Chef Style Famous Dressing, to taste

- Combine all ingredients.
- Toss and serve.
- Serves 4.

Honey Vegetable Salad

1 (16 oz) can green beans, drained
1½ cups fresh or frozen kernel corn
1½ cups fresh or frozen peas
1 (16 oz) can kidney beans or other beans, drained
1 cup celery, diced
1 green pepper, sliced
1 large onion, sliced in rings
salt to taste
dash of pepper
⅓ cup soybean oil
½ cup honey
¼ tsp dry mustard
⅔ cup Passport Seasonings Red Wine Vinegar
1 cup Morningland Dairy Cheese, any variety, cut in cubes

- In large bowl, combine vegetables, salt and pepper.
- Place oil, honey, mustard and wine vinegar in jar and shake to blend.
- Pour over vegetables.
- Cover and refrigerate overnight.
- Sprinkle cheese cubes over top of salad to serve.
- Serves 8-10.

Broccoli-Cauliflower Marinade

1 small head cauliflower, cut or broken into small flowerettes
1 small head broccoli, cut or broken into small flowerettes
1 small cucumber, sliced
1 small green pepper, cut into strips
1 small onion, cut and separated into rings, (optional)
2 cups cherry tomatoes left whole or large tomato cut in wedges
1 cup pitted black olives, (optional)
1 (16 oz) bottle Ott's Italian Dressing
salt and pepper to taste

- Toss raw vegetables to mix.
- Pour Ott's dressing over them and toss lightly 'til all pieces are covered.
- Marinate 8-12 hours in refrigerator in a covered container.
- Toss once or twice while marinating.
- Serves 6-8.

Missouri's Garden Greens

Look for AgriMissouri fresh produce in your market.

4 cups assorted greens, washed, dried and torn
½ cup red bell pepper, slivered
½ cup yellow bell pepper, slivered
½ cup red radish, thinly sliced
¼ cup fresh parsley, chopped
¼ cup green onions, slivered
½ cup asparagus, blanched and cut in diagonal slices, (optional)

- Toss all ingredients in a bowl.
- Serve with herb vinaigrette.
- Edible Flowers: such as, violets, nasturtiums, rose petals, oregano flowers or rosemary buds (optional)
- Greens: such as, leafy lettuce, bib lettuce, spinach, arugula, radicchio, Belgium endive.

Herb Vinaigrette

1 egg
or
2 tsp whipping cream
1 cup Hollywood Safflower Oil
⅓ cup Progresso Red Wine Vinegar
¾ tsp salt
½ tsp pepper
½ tsp garlic, minced
2 tbsp parsley, minced
1 tbsp fresh basil, minced
2 tbsp Herb Gathering Fresh Herbs, such as summer savory, thyme, oregano, dill, minced

- Whiz the egg and garlic in a food processor or whisk by hand with wire whip until lemon colored.
- Gradually add the oil so that it is well blended.
- Add remaining ingredients. Chill before using.
- Store in refrigerator.
- Makes 1½ cups.

Four-H has its roots in the farmland of America, and from Missouri 4-H records come interesting reports on gardening.

In the World War II year of 1943, Lloyd and Everett Koestler produced 18,536 plants, and sold these much-needed plants to their neighbors.

Leroy Block, in 1946 at age 9, supplied his family of 11 with fresh vegetbles from his garden. From the 12 different vegetables he planted, 400 quarts were canned for winter use.

Larry Hicks produced 20 tons of watermelons in Ray County in 1957 for an income of $175.

Eight 4-H clubs planted 8,000 trees along roadsides and around ponds in Cape Girardeau County in 1952.

The top crate of 4-H strawberries was sold by Larry Garrison of Jasper County in 1957 for $42.

Marinated Vegetables

1 small head cauliflower, broken into flowerettes
1 bunch broccoli, broken into flowerettes
2 green peppers, diced
2 medium onions, cut into large pieces
1 (16 oz) jar Old El Paso Thick 'n Chunky Salsa, Mild, Medium or Hot
1 cup distilled white vinegar
1 cup sugar
6 whole cloves
1 tsp allspice

- Blanch vegetables in boiling water for 5 minutes; drain.
- In a 2-qt saucepan over medium heat, combine salsa, vinegar, sugar, cloves and allspice.
- Bring to a boil; reduce heat and boil gently for 5 minutes.
- In clean, hot jars, alternate layers of broccoli, cauliflower, green peppers, and onions adding some of the marinade between each vegetable layer. Leave ½" head space at top of jar and seal.
- This vegetable marinade must be refrigerated.
- Yields 4 8-oz jars or 3 15-oz jars.

Creamy New Potato Salad

1 cup low-fat yogurt
1 cup Ott's Creamy Buttermilk Dressing
1 tbsp Dijon mustard
¼ cup dill weed, dried
8 cups small red, new potatoes, cooled and quartered
1 cup green pepper, diced
1 cup red onion, minced
1 cup celery, sliced
salt and pepper to taste

- In large bowl, combine low-fat yogurt and Ott's Creamy Buttermilk Dressing with Dijon mustard and dill weed.
- Add potatoes, green pepper, red onion and celery, and toss to combine.
- Add salt and pepper to taste.
- Cover and chill well.
- Serves 8-10.

Italian Potato Salad

8-10 medium red potatoes, cooked
1 large red onion, diced
salt to taste
pepper to taste
celery seed to taste
1 (8 oz) bottle Ott's Italian Dressing

- After potatoes have cooled enough to handle, peel and cube.
- Add diced onion, seasonings, dressing and mix well.
- Store in glass bowl and cover with plastic wrap for 6 hours for best flavor.
- Stir before serving.
- Serves 6.
- Will last several days in refrigerator.

An early-day settler plowed the fertile fields of Missouri's midsection and wrote back home to his family:

"Crops look promising and I do say I never saw such corn in my life. The stalks are so large that when we come to gathering it, we will have to take ladders to climb up to the ears.

"I am in a promised land where you have no need to work, for the land is so rich you may plant a crowbar at night and it will sprout 10 penny nails by morning."

'Better Than' Salad

3 cups Della Gourmet Rice, cooked
½ cup onion, finely chopped
1 cup Ott's Famous Dressing
1 tsp Aunt Joan's Ozark Mustard
2 hard-boiled eggs, chopped
¼ cup Aunt Nene's Sweet Pickle Relish
salt and pepper to taste

• Combine all ingredients.
• Mix thoroughly and chill.
• Serves 6.

Gazpacho Salad

8 medum tomatos, chopped
1 (16 oz) jar Old El Paso Thick 'n Chunky Salsa
¼ cup sherry wine or red wine vinegar
¼ cup red onions, chopped
¼ cup green onions, chopped
1 (4 oz) can Old El Paso Chopped Green Chilies, drained
4 cloves garlic, finely minced
2 cups cucumber, chopped into ¼" cubes
½ teaspoon coriander
2 tbsp dried basil
½ cup olive oil
salt and pepper
Old El Paso Nachips
Tortilla Chips

• In a large bowl, combine all ingredients except tortilla chips. Quantities of various ingredients may be varied according to taste.
• Chill, serve with tortilla chips.
• Serves 6-8.

Alumni of 4-H, more so than of any other group, have been recognized for the continued involvement in community activities.

As emphasized in the 4-H pledge, "for my club, my community, my country and my world," members have been active in

- victory gardens in the 40s
- urban gardens in the 60s
- covering open wells in the 80s

Insalata Di Pasta Primavera

1 lb Mangia Italiano Three-Color Fusilli Pasta
½ cup broccoli flowerettes
¼ cup olive oil
½ cup tomato wedges
½ cup onions, chopped coarse
½ cup zucchini halves, thinly sliced
½ cup celery, diced
½ cup red cabbage, finely shredded
¼ cup pickled red peppers, julienned
¼ cup green peppers, julienned
¼ cup parsley, chopped
¼ cup carrots, shredded
½ tsp salt
¼ tsp black pepper, fresh ground
⅛ cup lemon juice

- Bring to boil 4-5 qts of water in a 6-8 qt pot.
- Drop in fresh fusilli, stir quickly for 10 seconds then cook until al dente (approximately 3 minutes).
- Add the broccoli flowerettes and cook for another 30 seconds.
- Drain, rinse in cold water (to stop the cooking of the pasta) and drain again.
- Place the pasta in a large bowl, add the extra virgin olive oil and toss.
- Add all of the vegetables, salt and pepper and toss lightly again.
- Add the lemon juice and toss again.
- Serves 8.
- It will keep 2-3 days in the refrigerator, so it can be prepared ahead of time.

Pasta and Bean Salad

½ cup Progresso Olive Oil
3 tbsp Progresso Red Wine Vinegar
¾ teaspoon Italian seasoning
¼ tsp dry mustard
¼ tsp ground black pepper
¼ tsp sugar
⅛ tsp cayenne pepper
1 clove garlic, crushed
¼ cup Progresso Parmesan Cheese
½ lb corkscrew shape pasta, cooked and drained
1 (6 oz) jar Progresso Quartered Artichoke Hearts, drained
1 (10½ oz) can Progresso Chick Peas, drained
1 (10½ oz) can Progresso Red Kidney Beans, drained
2 stalks celery, sliced
2 medium tomatoes, cut in wedges

- In a blender, combine first 9 ingredients; set aside.
- In a large bowl, combine remaining ingredients.
- Pour reserved dressing over salad and toss gently.
- Refrigerate 2 hours or overnight.
- Serves 6-8.

Smoked Trout Salad

1 lb Mangia Italiano Rotini, (white, ¼" thick), cooked al dente
1 sweet red pepper, julienned
2 green onions, cut into ⅛" lengths
½ cup broccoli flowerettes, blanched
½ cup zucchini, sliced, blanched
1 red onion, sliced, blanched
3 tbsp capers, (small Spanish)
1 tsp parsley, finely diced
¼ tsp pepper
½ tsp salt
½ cup mayonnaise
2 smoked trout, skinned, boned and diced
1 lemon, juiced

- Combine pasta, vegetables and spices, toss with mayonnaise.
- Add trout and lemon juice, toss again.
- Garnish with parsley.

Once, not too long ago, Ozarkers held to folk beliefs that determined all planting patterns in their hills. They based many of their ideas on homespun astrology, handed down by generations. Yet their results always validated their methods. Ozark folklore played a major role in gardening until mass communication reached back into the hills, and scientific research was finally and cautiously accepted throughout the region.

Planting by the "dark of the moon" ensured best crop results for root vegetables: potatoes, carrots, peanuts, beets, onions, turnips, radishes, and the like. Potatoes could only be dug up by the light of the moon or they would rot in the ground. Planting by the "light of the moon" meant healthy beans, peas, corn and tomatoes.

Should fresh milk taste sour or chickens be hatched dead, the culprit was probably thunder.

And only on St. Valentine's Day could lettuce be planted.

Wilted Lettuce

lettuce
½ to ¾ cup sugar
¼ cup Passport Seasonings Vinegar
3 tbsp bacon drippings
salt and pepper

- Place leaf lettuce in large bowl, sprinkle sugar over lettuce.
- In a small sauce pan combine vinegar and bacon drippings and heat until boiling.
- Remove from heat, cool slightly before pouring over lettuce. Mix.
- Add salt and pepper as desired.

Ham and Vegetable Salad

½ of a 1 lb pkg elbow macaroni,
uncooked
2 cups Burger's Ham, cooked
and diced
1 medium red bell pepper,
chopped
1 medium yellow bell pepper,
chopped
1 medium cucumber, seeded
and chopped
2 cups fresh mushrooms, sliced
1 cup radishes, sliced
1 cup pitted ripe olives, sliced
½ cup red onion, chopped
¾ cup Italian dressing with
cheese and garlic
½ cup Cheddar cheese, shredded

- Prepare elbow macaroni according to package direction; drain.
- In medium bowl, combine all ingredients, except cheese.
- Cover; chill thoroughly.
- Toss salad gently before serving. Top with cheese.
- Serves 6-8.

Creamy Chicken Salad

½ of a 1 lb pkg corkscrew
noodles, uncooked
2 tbsp Hollywood Safflower Oil
2 tbsp Passport Seasoning
Vinegar
1 cup Hudson Chicken, cooked
and chopped
1 cup frozen peas, thawed and
drained
1 cup celery, chopped
½ cup Ott's Buttermilk Dressing
1 tbsp onion, finely chopped
½ tsp Andy's Seasoning salt
¼ tsp pepper

- Prepare corkscrew noodles according to package directions; drain.
- Combine noodles with oil and vinegar; toss to coat.
- Add remaining ingredients; toss gently to mix. Cover; chill thoroughly.
- Serves 4-6.

Missouri 4-H has continually added programs to enrich and contribute to the development of its young members. The state led the nation in the formulating of automotive care and safety projects for boys and girls. Developed by the agricultural engineering department of the University of Missouri, the programs were introduced in urban areas in the post-World War II years.

Photography was added as a project in the late 1950s, and immediately became popular with 4-H club members, rural and urban alike.

"You and Your Dog" and Outdoorsman were designed to meet the interest of youngsters living on farms as well as in small towns and cities. Child care was introduced in 1962, and was successfully implemented in both rural and urban areas.

Before 1960, without exception, 4-H work was concentrated in agriculture and home economics. In 1962, new pilot projects including small motors, general science, water safety, lawns, ham curing, rocks, pigeons, welding, library, guns and grain marketing were inaugurated. All projects placed emphasis on individual development, which continues to be the priority of 4-H work in Missouri today.

Layered Mexican Turkey Salad

1 lb Hudson Ground Turkey
1 (15 oz) can beans in chili sauce
¼ cup Old El Paso Thick 'n Chunky Salsa, Mild or Medium Hot
¼ tsp garlic powder
1 tsp chili powder
¼ tsp black pepper
2 cups lettuce pieces
2 cups Old El Paso Nachips Tortilla Chips, coarsely broken
1 cup Cheddar cheese, grated
1 cup tomatoes, seeded and chopped
¼ cup ripe olives, sliced

- In non-stick skillet, cook ground turkey until no longer pink, stirring to break up.
- Add beans, salsa, garlic powder, chili powder and pepper and heat until hot.
- Layer in salad bowl, or large platter, in order given, lettuce, tortilla chips, hot turkey mixture, cheese, tomatoes and olives.
- Use remaining salsa for salad dressing or use your favorite.
- Serves 4-6.

It was a cold and rainy early November day in 1943, and a gaggle of snow geese, soaring southward were framed against the autumn sky. Suddenly the geese broke out of their natural formation and dropped like leaves in a strong gust of wind. There were geese scattered on the ground as far as the eye could see.

Once the newswires picked up the story, reports flashed everywhere somewhat like the lightning which most folks think did the poor geese in. There were even two marriage proposals to a widowed Galena farm owner whose personal account of the number of dead geese on her land indicated her substantial property holdings.

Country Beef and Pasta Salad

1 (8 oz) pkg shell macaroni, cooked and drained
½ lb beef, cooked, thinly sliced and cut into strips
½ cup green onion including tops, sliced
½ cup ripe olives, sliced
¼ cup parsley, minced
12 cherry tomatoes, halved
½ cup Ott's Italian Salad Dressing

- Combine all ingredients in large bowl.
- Toss gently to coat with dressing.
- Cover and chill 3-4 hours or overnight.
- Serve as a cool main dish on a bed of crisp leaf lettuce.

Scandinavian Cucumbers

1 cup Hiland Sour Cream
1 tbsp red wine vinegar
2 tsp sugar
1 tsp salt
2 medium cucumbers, sliced
1 medium red onion, sliced

- Combine sour cream, vinegar, sugar and salt, mix well.
- Add combined cucumbers and onions; mix lightly.
- Chill. Toss just before serving.
- Serves 6-8.

Missouri has always depended on gifts from the good earth, as well as on its own ingenuity.

Times were hard.

Living wasn't always easy.

But Missouri didn't complain.

It just rolled up its sleeves, went to work, and was eternally grateful for what it received, as depicted in the words of a settler in the 1850s.

"All the corn we make our bread of groweth on our own ground. The flesh we eat is all, or the most part, of our own breeding. Our garments, also or much thereof, are made within our house. Our own malt and water maketh our drink.

"We have corn in the granary, cheese in the loft, milk in the dairy, cream in the pot, butter in the dish, ale in the tub, beef in the brine, bacon in the attic, herbs in the garden, and water at our door.

"What in God's name can we desire to have more."

Light Salad

1 (3 oz) pkg lemon gelatin
1 (3 oz) pkg lime gelatin
1 can Pet Light Evaporated Skimmed Milk
1 cup mayonnaise, Light
1 cup Glamour Low-Fat Cottage Cheese
1 16 oz can pineapple, crushed, (leave in own juice)
¾ cup Byrd's Pecans
2 Missouri Apples, grated

- Use 1 cup boiling water to dissolve each flavor of gelatin.
- Mix in remaining ingredients and refrigerate overnight or until set (5-6 hours).
- Serves 10.

Breads

Berry Connection Muffin Favorite

2 cups self-rising flour
½ cup sugar
1½ cups Missouri Blueberries
½ cup pecans or walnuts,
chopped
½ cup coconut
½ cup oats
4 eggs
1 cup Fairmont Milk
¼ cup soybean oil
¼ cup Mid-American Farms
Sour Cream

- Preheat oven to 425 degrees.
- In a large bowl combine all dry ingredients
- Stir in blueberries, nuts, coconut, and oats.
- In a small bowl beat eggs; stir in milk, oil and sour cream just until blended.
- Make a well in center of dry ingredients and mix until dry ingredients are blended. Do not over mix.
- Fill muffin tins and bake for 15-20 minutes.
- Makes 24 small or 12 large muffins.

A list for medicinal cures found at scattered outposts along the Missouri frontier would read somewhat like bottles of quinine, rhubarb juice, castor oils, and, of course, a goodly amount of whiskey. Medicine was a composite of herbal mixtures and good fortune.

The Indians relied on a wealth of herbal pharmacopoeia. They knew that a potion using the common field daisy, when boiled in water and ingested, would prevent ague or malarial fever in its earliest stages. A tea made from sassafras tree leaves was a most effective palliative. Tree bark and fruit belonged to the tribal cures. Wild yarrow grew throughout Missouri and was used to wash out blood impurities and prevent colds. Savory when rubbed on the skin repelled the summer's mosquitoes.

Southwest Missouri Blueberry Cream Cheese Muffins

1 cup Missouri Blueberries
2 cups flour
¾ cup sugar
1½ tsp baking powder
3 oz cream cheese
2 tsp lemon juice
½ cup Fairmont Milk
¼ cup butter, melted
2 eggs
2 tsp vanilla
Pinch of salt

- Toss blueberries with 2 tbsp flour; set aside.
- Combine remaining dry ingredients; set aside.
- With blade in food processor blend cheese, lemon juice, milk and butter.
- Add eggs, pulse 4-5 times.
- Add flour, pulse 6 times.
- Stir in blueberries by hand.
- Fill greased muffin cups ⅔ full.
- Bake at 400 degrees 18-20 minutes.

Mid-America Dairymen Inc., headquartered in Springfield, Missouri, was organized in 1967 by the consolidation of three regional dairy cooperatives in Kansas and Missouri. Since then, as a result of additional mergers, acquisitions and consolidations, Mid-America Dairymen now represents approximately 9,700 dairy farmers in the states of North and South Dakota, Minnesota, Wisconsin, Nebraska, Iowa, Illinois, Missouri, Kansas, Arkansas, Oklahoma and Texas.

Eight Missouri plants manufacture or process a variety of Mid-Am products:

Springfield - Infant formula, butter and dehydrated products, as well as Hiland Dairy fluid milk and ice cream.

Cabool - Infant formula and Sport Shake (the only product of its kind on the market).

Chillicothe - Mozzarella cheese.

Eldorado Springs - Cottage cheese and dehydrated products.

Lebanon - Sour cream, dips, yogurts, coffee creamers, whipping cream.

Mt. Vernon - Mozzarella cheese.

Clinton - Processed American cheese.

In Kansas City, Fairmont-Zarda Dairy is a wholly-owned subsidiary of Mid-America Dairymen, Inc. It processes a complete line of fluid dairy products, including whole, lowfat and skim milk, and flavored milk drinks under the Fairmont-Zarda label. Fairmont services the retail and food trade in a 100-mile radius of Kansas City.

Broccoli Cornbread

2 sticks Mid-America Farms Butter
1 tsp dried or fresh onion, (optional)
2 (8½ oz) boxes corn muffin mix
4 eggs
1 cup Mid-America Farms Cottage Cheese
1 (10 oz) box frozen chopped broccoli

- Melt butter in 9"x13" pan.
- Mix all ingredients together. Spoon mixture into pan with melted butter.
- Bake according to instructions on corn muffin box. (May need to bake longer.)

Double Cheese Apple Muffins

1½ cups flour
½ cup yellow cornmeal
½ cup Missouri Apples, chopped
¼ cup brown sugar, firmly packed
1 tbsp baking powder
¾ tsp cinnamon
1 cup Fairmont Milk
2 eggs, beaten
½ cup cream-style Mid-America Farms Cottage Cheese
¼ cup butter, melted
½ cup Mid-America Farms Cheddar Cheese, shredded

- Preheat oven to 400 degrees.
- Combine flour, cornmeal, apples, sugar, baking powder and cinnamon in a large mixing bowl.
- Stir liquid ingredients into dry ingredients just until combined.
- Fill buttered muffin cups ⅔ full.
- Bake 20-25 minutes.
- Serve warm with butter.
- Yields about 18 muffins.

Pumpkin Bread

1 can (16 oz) pumpkin
4 eggs
1 cup soybean oil
⅔ cup orange juice
3½ cups flour
3 cups sugar
2 tsp baking soda
½ tsp salt
4 tsp pumpkin pie spice

- Preheat oven to 350 degrees.
- In large bowl mix pumpkin, eggs, oil and juice until well blended.
- Sift together flour, sugar, baking soda, salt and pumpkin pie spice.
- Add sifted dry ingredients to pumpkin mixture. Beat until smooth.
- Pour batter into 2 greased and floured loaf pans, 9⅝"x5½"x2¾".
- Bake at 350 degrees for 1 hour or until bread tests done.
- Remove bread from pans and cool on a wire rack.
- Makes two loaves.

If the soybean were a person, one would say it is very modest or secretive. But the shy legume is rapidly becoming one of our most important diet components, primarily because of the bean's ability to be converted into low-fat, low-cholesterol foodstuffs.

Soybeans, in some form, can be found in a multitude of food products: bread, candy, pie crust, crackers, coffee creamers, cooking oils, salad dressings, sandwich spreads, shortenings, milk, margarine, mayonnaise, chocolate, instant mixes, cereals, noodles, pizzas, beer, ale, meat products, baby food, diet foods, and frozen desserts.

The Chinese were the first to discover the versatile soybean about 5,000 years ago, calling it "Yellow Jewel" and "Great Treasure." Peasants planted the seeds of a wild plant, and by 1100 B.C. the plant began producing larger seeds. From these seeds, the Chinese created bean sprouts, sauces, flour, cooking oil and milk, which gave soybeans the name "cow of China." The most important soybean contribution to the diet of the Chinese was in the form of bean curd, or doufu, used as a meat substitute. Soybeans are regarded as the most important crop, one of five sacred grains they couldn't live without.

Granny's Sweet Potato Bread

1 cup soybean oil
2 cups sugar
4 eggs
2 cups sweet potatoes, cooked, mashed
⅔ cup water
3½ cups flour
2 tsp soda
2 tsp salt
1 tsp allspice
½ tsp cloves
1 tsp nutmeg
1 tsp cinnamon
1½ cups oatmeal
1 cup raisins

- Cream oil and sugar.
- Add eggs and sweet potatoes, mix well.
- Sift dry ingredients, add a little at a time to the sugar-egg mixture, alternating with water.
- Add oatmeal and raisins.
- Divide dough between 2 9"x5" loaf pans.
- Bake at 325 degrees for 1 hour or until done.
- Makes 2 loaves.

Honey Wheat Rolls

½ cup butter or margarine
½ cup Gibbons
Wildflower Honey
½ tsp salt
2 tbsp potato flakes
1 cup hot water
2 pkgs active dry yeast
½ cup lukewarm water
4½ cups sifted flour
(½ all-purpose, ½ whole wheat)
melted butter or margarine

- Combine butter, honey, salt, potato flakes and hot water in bowl. Cool to lukewarm.
- Sprinkle yeast on lukewarm water; stir to dissolve. Add yeast mixture and 1 cup flour to potato mixture.
- Beat with electric mixer at medium speed until smooth, about 2 minutes, scraping bowl occasionally.
- Gradually add enough remaining flour to make a soft dough that leaves the sides of the bowl.
- Place dough in greased bowl; turn over to grease top. Cover and let rise in warm place until doubled, about 1¼ hours.
- Turn dough onto lightly floured surface. Divide dough into 24 pieces. Shape each piece into a ball. Place in greased baking pans. Let rise until doubled, about 45 minutes.
- Bake in 375 degree oven 20 minutes or until golden brown. Brush with honey glaze or melted butter.
- Makes 24 rolls.

Honey Glaze for Wheat Rolls:

¼ cup butter or margarine
1 egg white
½ cup powdered sugar
¼ cup Gibbons
Wildflower Honey

- Melt butter and cool slightly.
- Blend in remaining ingredients.
- As soon as rolls are removed from oven, brush with glaze. Let set a few minutes.

Pierre de Laclede Liguest, a Frenchman of breeding and education, and a major player in the fur trade, came up the Mississippi from New Orleans, settling at a spot on its west bank in 1764 and naming the patch of ground Saint Louis.

His stepson, Auguste Chouteau, quoted Laclede in his journal: "I have found a site on which to form my settlement which might hereafter become one of the finest cities in America."

To say Laclede was a visionary is perhaps too mild a commentary.

Savory Bread Sticks

1 loaf of a Butternut White Bread, crusts removed
½ cup soybean oil margarine, softened
1 tsp garlic salt
1 tsp onion salt
½ cup Parmesan cheese
2 tsp dill weed

- Preheat oven to 350 degrees.
- Arrange bread slices in jelly roll pan 15½"x10½"x1".
- Spread softened margarine evenly over bread.
- Sprinkle with garlic and onion salt, cheese and dill weed.
- Bake for 10 minutes. Then cut into strips using kitchen shears.
- Return to 350 degrees oven and continue baking approximately 20 minutes, until breadsticks are evenly browned a light golden color.
- Cool completely before storing in airtight containers.
- If you would like to cut the bread sticks before baking — freeze the bread. Then cut with a sharp knife while frozen. Total baking time is approximately 30 minutes.

The American breakfast food industry can thank an entrepreneurial mind in St. Joseph for creating pancake mix. This simple yet sophisticated advancement in food production was a self-rising pancake flour that was packaged and sold in the late nineteenth century.

One of the inventors in 1893 saw a comedian imitating a southern plantation mammy, wearing a cooking apron and red bandana. The comedian sang a song entitled, "Aunt Jemima." From this came the introduction of Aunt Jemima pancakes at the Chicago World's Fair. The rest, as they say, is history.

Eggnog French Toast

Holiday recipe to be made ahead and frozen.

3 eggs
1 cup eggnog
2 tsp granulated sugar
½ tsp vanilla extract
⅛ tsp ground nutmeg
pinch salt
8 slices Nancy Anne White or Whole Wheat Bread
butter or margarine, melted
syrup or jam

- In a medium size mixing bowl, beat eggs slightly.
- Add eggnog, sugar, vanilla, nutmeg and salt. Beat well.
- Soak each slice of bread in egg mixture and place on a well-greased baking sheet. Cover baking sheet with foil and place in freezer until bread is completely frozen.

To Store:
- Stack frozen bread slices, placing a sheet of waxed paper between each slice; wrap stack in foil. Store in freezer.

To Cook:
- Remove desired number of bread slices from freezer. Brush one side of each slice with melted butter.
- Place bread, buttered side down, on an ungreased baking sheet.
- Bake in a preheated 425 degree oven 10 minutes.
- Brush top of each slice with melted butter and turn over with a pancake turner so that buttered side is down.
- Bake until toast is golden brown, 5 to 10 minutes more.
- Serve with syrup or jam.
- Serves 8.

Across the Missouri landscape are more than 113,000 farms, producing corn and soybeans in the northern fields and cotton and rice in the delta lands of the southeast. Beef and dairy enterprises sprawl throughout the Ozarks.

Seven percent of the U.S. soybeans and grain sorghum is grown in Missouri, and six percent of the U.S. turkeys is raised in the state.

Missouri is the second leading state in beef cows and the second leading state in hay production. It ranks sixth in rice production, seventh in all wheat and corn production, tenth in cotton production, and twelfth in red meat production.

Missouri is the eleventh leading state in milk production. Six percent of the U.S. cattle operations and five percent of the U.S. hog operations are located in the state.

Rhubarb Nut Bread

½ cup Mid-America Farms
Butter, (1 stick)
1 cup sugar
1 tbsp grated orange peel
1 tsp vanilla extract
2 eggs
2½ cups flour
1 tsp baking soda
¼ tsp salt
¾ cup buttermilk
1½ cup fresh or frozen rhubarb,
coarsely chopped
¾ cup pecans or walnuts,
chopped

- Preheat oven to 350 degrees.
- Butter bottom only of 9"x5" loaf pan, set aside.
- Beat butter, sugar, orange peel and vanilla in large mixer bowl until light and fluffy.

- Add eggs, one at a time, beating well after each addition.
- Add 2¼ cups flour and remaining dry ingredients alternately with buttermilk to butter mixture, beating at low speed just until blended.
- Toss rhubarb with remaining ¼ cup flour, fold into batter with nuts.
- Turn into prepared pan, spreading evenly.
- Bake until wooden pick inserted in center comes out clean, about 1 hour and 20 minutes.
- Cool in pan 10 minutes.
- Remove from pan and cool completely on wire rack.
- Makes one loaf.

Sandwiches

Blarney Corned Beef Sandwich

1 tbsp thousand island dressing
2 slices pumpernickel bread
1 tbsp cream horseradish
2½ oz Boyle's Famous Corned Beef, cooked and sliced paper thin
2 thin slices of onion
2 thin slices of tomato
2 oz wilted spinach or creamy coleslaw
1 tbsp butter or margarine
ripe olives, marinated cucumber slices, dill spears to garnish.

- Spread dressing on one slice of bread, and horseradish on the other slice.
- Place corned beef, onion, tomato and spinach or coleslaw between slices.
- Butter outer sides of bread.
- Grill in 350 degree oven until golden brown.
- Garnish with ripe olives, cucumber slices, or crisp dill spears.
- Serves 1.

Little known facts about corned beef from Boyle's Famous Corned Beef Company:

- The Romans were the first to discover corned beef's tastiness and resistance to spoilage. On long campaigns in Britain and Gaul, it was a welcome addition to their meals.

- Though they were not the first, the Irish adopted the tasty meat as their own.

- The word "corned" originally designated meat preserved by dry salting instead of brining. A "corn" of salt was simply a grain of coarse salt.

- The advent of refrigeration changed the methods of processing corned beef. Now the fat is trimmed away and a rare spice blend is injected into the meat before being wrapped in a clear plastic.

- Corned beef can be substituted in a variety of recipes to add zip and taste appeal.

- Versatile and adaptable, corned beef enjoys continuing popularity.

Creamy Cheesy Corned Beef Sandwiches

2 oz Philadelphia Brand®
Cream Cheese
2 tbsp Walker's Horseradish
dash hot pepper sauce
8 slices Jewish rye bread
8 oz Boyle's Famous Corned
Beef, sliced very thin
4 (1 oz) slices of Swiss cheese
3 tbsp butter

- Blend together cream cheese, horseradish and hot pepper sauce.
- Spread on one side of bread slices.
- Layer 2 oz corned beef and 1 oz Swiss cheese. Close sandwich.
- Spread outside with butter.
- Grill until cheese is melted.
- Serves 4.

The War Between the States tore Missouri apart.

Only Virginia and Tennessee witnessed more skirmishes than did Missouri.

And the state furnished more calvarymen for the Union forces than any other state except New York. In fact, Missouri put more battalions, companies and regiments in the field than any other northern state.

The Blue had 109,000 Missourians in its ranks.

The Confederacy had 30,000.

And 60 percent of the men of Missouri who were eligible for service chose to fight in the war. More than 20,000 of them died.

Broiled Irish Reubenburger

¼ cup onion, chopped
½ cup soybean oil
1½ lbs Boyle's Famous Corned Beef, cooked and ground
1 tbsp Walker's Horseradish, cream style
½ tsp salt
2 eggs
7 oz bread crumbs, divided
butter, softened
6 rye buns
6 slices Mid-America Swiss Cheese
6 oz sauerkraut, drained

- Saute onion in 1 tbsp oil until transparent.
- Combine corned beef, onions, horseradish, salt, eggs, and ½ cup bread crumbs.
- Shape into 4″ patties (6 patties).
- Coat patties lightly in remaining bread crumbs.
- Place remaining oil in skillet over medium heat.
- Cook patties until golden brown on 1 side. Turn and lightly brown other side.
- Lightly butter cut sides of bun halves and toast to light brown.
- On bottom toasted rye bun half, place 1 corned beef patty and top with slice of Swiss cheese.
- On top toasted rye bun half, place 1 oz of drained sauerkraut.
- Place in 350 degree oven or under broiler until cheese is soft and melting.
- Serve open-face.
- Serves 6.

Four-H members have long been interested in wildlife, and Melvin Wahl, Warren County, recalled:

"In the winter of 1939-1940 I fed 40 quail at two stations. One of the stations was a low bushy cedar tree and the other was a hog house under a bushy oak tree. I had trouble with the foxes catching the quail when they were in their shelters.

"I kept traps for the foxes but did not succeed in catching one. Later I demonstrated a system that would provide ample food, cover and water for two club groups and two farm groups in the community. There are now twice as many quail on the farm as when I first tried to shelter and feed them."

Erin's Best

3 slices round rye with poppy seed
3 oz Boyle's Corned Beef
1½ oz white cabbage, minced
dash white pepper
salt to taste
2 Aunt Nene's Zesty Sweet Dill Slices
2 ripe black olives

Erin's Spread:
½ tsp prepared mustard
½ tsp Walker's Horseradish
1 tsp mayonnaise
2 tbsp cream cheese
2 tbsp Mid-America Farms Sour Cream
salt and pepper, to taste

- First, prepare Erin's Spread by mixing all the ingredients in a small bowl. Set aside.
- Butter bread lightly and grill or toast — Do not remove crusts.
- Cover one side of bread with Erin's Spread and top with 1½ oz of corned beef.
- Combine cabbage with salt and pepper.
- Spread ¾ oz of the raw minced white cabbage over the corned beef. Spread second slice of bread on both sides with Erin's Spread and place on raw minced white cabbage.
- Add the remaining 1½ oz of corned beef atop second slice of bread and top with remainder of minced cabbage.
- Slice sandwich in 2 pieces.
- Garnish with dill slices and ripe olives.

In 1914, A. J. Seitz founded Seitz Foods Inc. of St. Joseph, Missouri, becoming a major meat producer and community leader.

Rick Benward, director of sales, states, "I think anything that provides youth with proper guidance in their lifestyle choices toward preventing problems is important.

"We salute the 4-H community for their foresight. We are dependent on their efforts and the results of their efforts for the raw material product necessary to produce the end product for consumers of Missouri."

Seitz manufactures a variety of luncheon meats, smoked sausages, smokey links, polish sausage, kielbasa and hot dogs, including meat, beef and lower salt varieties. Sliced ham and turkey in several flavors round out Seitz's product line, along with chili and bacon.

Seitz specialty bologna is processed in 10 varieties: meat, beef, cheese, jalapeno, thick, thin, garlic, mild, lower salt meat and lower salt beef.

Amazingly, Seitz can manufacture 56,600 hot dogs in one hour! In one year, Seitz produces more than seven million pounds of hot dogs, enough to fill 200 semi trucks for delivery. End to end, it takes 12,672 hot dogs to stretch one mile!

From the 14 million pounds of lunch meat produced by Seitz each year, 163,000,000 sandwiches can be made!

Best Hamdogs

1 cup Seitz Cooked Ham or Seitz Luncheon Meat, finely chopped
3 tbsp pickle relish
2 tbsp onions, finely chopped
2 tbsp prepared mustard
2 tbsp mayonnaise
1 lb Seitz Hot Dogs
8 slices of bacon
Missouri Classic Barbecue Sauce, as needed

- Mix first 5 ingredients.
- Slit hot dogs, cutting almost to ends and only ¾ the way through.
- Stuff with ham mixture. Wrap with bacon and secure with wooden picks.
- Broil over hot coals brushing with sauce until filling is hot and bacon crisp.
- Serve in toasted buns.
- Serves 8.

Microwave Hot Hero Sandwiches

2 (½ lb) mini loaves
French bread
butter or margarine
2 cups (8 oz) Morningland Dairy
Cheddar Cheese, shredded
1 cup Seitz Salami, chopped
½ cup mayonnaise
¼ cup onion, chopped
¼ cup ripe olives, sliced
2 tbsp prepared mustard

- Slice each French loaf horizontally in half, then crosswise in thirds.
- Butter slices of bread.
- Combine remaining ingredients for filling on bread and wrap each sandwich in a paper towel.
- Heat 3 sandwiches at a time in microwave oven until hot. (2½-3 minutes on high).
- Serves 6.

A Nancy Anne Hero

1 (14"-15") loaf Nancy Anne
French Bread
¼ cup chili sauce
¼ cup mayonnaise
2 tsp prepared horseradish
1 cup shredded iceberg lettuce
½ small green or red pepper, cut
into thin strips
⅓ lb thinly sliced turkey
⅓ lb baby Swiss cheese
⅓ lb thinly sliced ham

- Cut bread in half, lengthwise.
- Combine chili sauce, mayonnaise and horseradish. Spread half of mixture over bottom half of bread.
- Spread lettuce and pepper strips over sauce mixture on bread.
- Layer on turkey, cheese and ham.
- Spoon remaining sauce mixture over top.
- Put top piece of bread over ingredients making a sandwich.
- Serves 4.

Siciliano Muffeletta Sandwich

1 round Italian bread
with sesame seeds,
(about 9" in diameter)
1 cup prepared olive salad,
Sicilian antipasto,
or olive condite
8 thin slices Volpi
Genova Salame
4 slices Provolone cheese
(or Swiss)
3 slices Volpi Prosciutto, thin
2 slices Volpi Mortadella, thin

- Slice bread in half (across the diameter) and brush each half with some of the oil from the olive salad or salad oil.
- On half of the bread, place 4 slices of the Genova Salame, top with the Provolone, Prosciutto, Mortadella and the remaining Genova Salame.
- Spread the olive salad over the salami and top with bread.
- Cut into quarters and serve.

Note: This sandwich should not be heated.

Pita Pockets

2 slices whole wheat pita bread,
cut in half
8 oz Hudson Smoked Turkey or
Turkey Ham, thinly sliced
1 cup cucumbers, thinly sliced
¼ cup red onion, minced
1 cup tomato, chopped and
seeded
1 cup alfalfa sprouts
½ cup Ott's Creamy
Buttermilk Dressing

- Divide and arrange all ingredients among the pita pocket halves.
- Drizzle with dressing.
- Serve immediately.
- Serves 4.

Throughout Missouri are the homes of its famous native sons and daughters.

The George Caleb Bingham House is located at Arrow Rock, where the Santa Fe Trail crossed the Missouri River.

Harry S. Truman's birthplace can be found in Lamar, his office in Independence.

John J. Pershing's boyhood home is the pride of Laclede.

Thomas Hart Benton resided in Kansas City, where his home and carriage house are now a State Historic Site.

Jesse James' Birthplace, a pre-Civil War mansion, overlooks Kearney. In St. Joseph, however, is the home where the notorious outlaw was killed.

At her home in Mansfield, Laura Ingalls Wilder wrote her Little House on The Prairie books.

Within the privacy of his St. Louis home, Eugene Field created the beautiful poetry that earned him the title, "The Children's Poet."

Chicken Salad En Croute

1 (1 lb) Italian bread loaf
2 cups Hudson Chicken, cooked and chopped
1 cup grape halves
½ cup mayonnaise
½ cup celery, chopped
¼ cup slivered almonds, toasted
1 tbsp onion, chopped
1 tbsp lemon juice
½ tsp curry powder
½ lb Velveeta® Pasteurized Process Cheese Spread, cubed

- Preheat oven to 350 degrees.
- Cut lengthwise slice ½" from top of bread loaf; remove center, leaving ½" shell.
- Tear removed bread into bite-sized pieces; combine with all remaining ingredients except cheese spread.
- Fill shell with half of cheese spread; top cheese with half of chicken mixture; repeat layers.
- Cover with top of bread loaf; wrap in foil.
- Bake 55 minutes.
- Serves 8.

Fruit 'N Cheesy Grill

½ cup pitted dates, chopped
½ cup Missouri Dandy
Black Walnuts, chopped
½ cup raisins
½ cup Kraft® Light Mayonnaise
8 slices Butternut Whole Wheat
Bread
8 slices process cheese spread
butter, softened

- Mix dates, walnuts, raisins and mayonnaise.
- For each sandwich, cover one bread slice with one process cheese spread slice, ⅓ cup mayonnaise mixture, second process cheese spread slice and second bread slice.
- Spread sandwich with butter.
- Grill until lightly browned on both sides.
- Serves 4.

Pocket Italian Sandwich

1½ lbs lean Missouri Beef,
(sirloin tip roast is good to use.)
1 (8 oz) bottle Ott's
Italian Dressing
¼ cup soybean oil
1 pkg pocket bread
1 onion, chopped
2 tomatoes, chopped
6 lettuce leaves
1 cup cheese, grated

- Cut thin slices of beef. Place in shallow dish.
- Pour Italian dressing to generously cover meat. Marinate in refrigerator for several hours or overnight.
- Remove slices of beef from dressing and fry in oil until tender. Do not overcook.
- Prepare pocket bread as directed on package.
- Place a few slices of cooked beef in pocket bread.
- Add chopped onion, tomato, lettuce and grated cheddar cheese.
- Serve promptly.
- Serves 6.

Ivan Strickler, a Missouri dairyman, once sold his milk to a proprietary organization. He owned a can milk route, picking up other farmers' milk and delivering it to a collection facility along with his own.

One day, the manager of the facility informed Ivan that he would no longer be able to receive his milk. Ivan was bewildered. Was the quality bad? Had he done anything wrong? No, the manager explained, it was simply a matter of having too much milk. "Either you cut-off several smaller producers and have them all mad at you," Ivan was told, "or you cut-off one large producer and risk his anger."

Ivan had no place to market his milk. It was at this time that he became involved with a dairy cooperative, an organization of dairy farmers who collectively joined together to sell all the milk they produced at the highest possible return.

Now Ivan Strickler is president of Mid-America Dairymen Inc. which encourages the individual to market his milk through a dairy marketing cooperative, hopefully through Mid-America Dairymen.

Layered Ham Brunch Muffins

2 cups Mid-America Farms Sour Cream
1 cup mayonnaise
1 tbsp Dijon mustard
2 tsp curry powder
6 English muffins, split and toasted
12 slices Farmland "Our Special Cut" Pre-Sliced Ham
8 hard-cooked eggs, sliced
12 slices fresh or canned pineapple, well drained

Note: May be assembled ahead and refrigerated until ready to bake.

- Combine sour cream, mayonnaise, Dijon mustard and curry powder.
- Spread one tbsp of mixture on each toasted muffin half.
- Place English muffins, cut side up, in 2 baking pans.
- Cut ham slices in half; place 2 halves on each muffin.
- Top each ham slice with 4 egg slices and a slice of pineapple.
- Spread remaining sour cream mixture on pineapple slices.
- Bake, covered, at 325 degrees for 20-30 minutes.
- Serves 6.

4-H has always striven to provide practical education to motivate youths to be productive. Because rural Missouri was so far behind the more progressive urban areas, 4-H emphasized projects that required youngsters to produce. The first year, club work was limited to corn projects for boys and tomato projects for girls. Soon the boys began raising pigs and calves, and the girls were "cold pack" canning their tomato crops.

Extension agents, armed with the latest knowledge of crop and livestock production, soon found the easiest way to reach adults was through their children enrolled in club work. Thus, 4-H became a valuable teaching tool to communicate with Missouri farmers.

Smoked Sausage Sandwiches

1 lb Farmland Lower Salt Smoked Sausage
¼ cup orange juice
1 tsp dried oregano leaves
1 red onion, quartered
2 green bell peppers, seeded and cut into ½" thick strips
3 pita bread rounds, cut in half
green leaf lettuce
½ cup Mid-America Farms Colby Cheese, shredded
½ cup Mid-America Farms Monterey Jack Cheese, shredded
brown spicy mustard to taste

- Light outdoor grill.
- Diagonal-cut smoked sausage into 30 ½" thick slices.
- Combine orange juice and oregano in a small bowl. Stir well.
- Separate layers of red onion quarters.

- Place sausage, onion and bell peppers alternately on 6 metal skewers. Brush with orange juice mixture.
- Place skewers on grill and cook, covered, at moderate heat for 6-8 minutes or until vegetables are tender, but crisp, and sausage is thoroughly heated. Turn skewers frequently and baste with orange juice mixture.
- Near the end of grilling time, set pita halves on the grill to warm.
- Remove skewers and bread from grill. Line pita with lettuce. Slide kabob from skewers into pita pockets.
- Sprinkle tops with cheese, and serve with brown spicy mustard.
- Serves 6.

Bagels are known, quite simply, as a roll with a hole.

Golden brown and crusty, they are low in calories, with a three-ounce bagel containing only 270 calories.

The world saw its first bagel in 1683 when a baker decided to develop something new as a tribute to Jan Sobretsky, the King of Poland, who had just saved the people of Austria from the onslaught of Turkish invaders.

Since the King was a noted horseman, the baker shaped the yeast dough into an uneven circle resembling a stirrup. The Austrian word for stirrup, in fact, is beugel.

West Coast Health Bagel

2 Petrofsky's Wheat Bagels
cream cheese
1 ripe avocado, mashed
alfalfa sprouts
1 onion, sliced
1 tomato, sliced

- Slice bagels in half and spread with softened cream cheese.
- Top with mashed avocado, alfalfa sprouts, sliced onion and tomatoes.
- Serves 2.

Tally-Ho Rarebit

2 Petrofsky's Pumpernickel Bagels
1 tomato, sliced
12 oz Morningland Dairy Cheddar Cheese
⅛ tsp prepared mustard
dash of cayenne pepper
dash of Worcestershire sauce
1 can ale

- Slice bagels in half.
- Top each with tomato slice.
- Melt and heat cheese, mustard, cayenne pepper, Worcestershire sauce and ale.
- Cook until smooth.
- Cover each bagel half with sauce.
- Serves 2.

Main Dishes

St. Louis Cardinals Stew

2½ lbs lean Missouri Beef Stew
Meat, cut in chunks
salt and pepper to taste
6 medium potatoes, quartered
6 medium carrots, coarsely sliced
1 large onion, diced
1 cup celery, cut up
1 tsp Andy's Seasoning Salt
2 tbsp brown sugar
3 tbsp tapioca
1 tbsp Worcestershire sauce
1½-2 cups tomato juice

- Put all ingredients into a large covered Dutch oven or heavy casserole dish.
- Bake at 300 degrees for 3-4 hours until beef is tender.
- Serves 6.

Corned Beef Hash

1 tbsp bacon fat
1 small garlic clove
¾ lb cooked Boyle's Famous
Corned Beef, diced
3 small green onions, chopped
1 tomato, chopped
2 medium potatoes, diced
and cooked
1 tsp. Worcestershire sauce
2 oz. Hermannof Norton
Dry Red Wine

- Add minced garlic to bacon fat and brown slightly in skillet.
- Add remaining ingredients and cook until heated through.
- For a crisp crust, don't stir. Turn out on platter with crisp side up.
- Serves 2.

Robert W. Boyle founded Boyle's Famous Corned Beef Company in 1954 with just one product, a raw corned beef brisket. In the beginning, the meat was merchandised through one Kansas City distributor. Now there is a full network of distributors and brokers covering the 50 states and 10 foreign countries.

To keep up with demand, Boyle's has added a cooked ready-to-serve corned beef brisket, and a cooked and hickory smoked brisket. His first cooker accepted just two briskets at a time, and daily output was about 500 pounds. Current production is at 20,000 pounds per day.

Boyle reflects on his years as a 4-H member:

"I was a member of 4-H in 1926 at Mexico, Missouri, High School in Audrain Country and was on the first 4-H beef judging team that the school sponsored. Our instructor was A. Gorrell, who later became principal of the school.

"I'm still using knowledge learned in that beef judging period in this business today."

"I'm very proud of my 4-H experience and still call on those memories."

Onion-Crusted Corned Beef Hash Casserole

4 cups onions, sliced
3 tbsp salad oil
1½ lbs cooked Boyle's Famous Corned Beef, chopped
½ lb cooked potatoes, chopped
½ tsp Worcestershire sauce
½ tsp salt, (optional)
¾ tsp pepper
6 tbsp milk
½ tsp curry powder
½ cup bread crumbs
½ cup Morningland Dairy Cheddar Cheese, grated

- Preheat oven to 400 degrees.
- Saute onions in oil until crisp and golden brown.
- Combine potatoes and corned beef and arrange in 10"x16"x2" baking dish.
- Add Worcestershire sauce, salt and pepper. Toss with fork until mixed.
- Even out hash mixture and pour milk over it.
- Add curry to onions, mix well and arrange over hash.
- Toss bread crumbs mixed with cheese over onions.
- Bake for 20 minutes.
- Serves 6.

Robert Boyle's father, Peter Simon Boyle, was one of the stone masons that built the memorial tower at the University of Missouri, Columbia. Only a youngster then, Bob was a water boy for those stone masons.

Corned Beef Dinner

3-3½ lbs Boyles Famous Corned Beef Brisket
2 medium onions, sliced
2 cloves garlic, minced
3 medium carrots, cut in ½" chunks
3 medium potatoes, pared and quartered
1½ lbs cabbage, cut in wedges
3 bay leaves
1 cup water
1 tbsp mustard
⅓ cup brown sugar

- Place all vegetables and bay leaves in slow cooker.
- Add brisket and water.
- Cover and cook on low heat setting for 10 hours.
- The last hour remove bay leaves and spread mustard and brown sugar over meat.
- Garnish with parsley.
- Serves 5-6.

Beef Brisket

1 (16 oz) jar Old El Paso
Picante Sauce
1 can beer
1 pkg dry onion soup mix
1 Missouri Beef Brisket

- Mix together first 3 ingredients and pour over brisket.
- Cover and bake 2½-3 hours in 350 degree oven. Uncover last ½ hour.

Steak Shiitake

4 (8 oz) Missouri Beef Filets
1 (8 oz) jar Persimmon Hill
Shiitake Mushroom Sauce
salt and pepper to taste

- Grill filets 3-5 inches above the coals. Grill about 15 minutes, turning once, or to desired doneness.
- Season with salt and pepper.
- Heat Shiitake Mushroom Sauce and serve on top of steaks.
- Serves 4.

Herbed Beef Roast

8 lb Missouri Beef Rib Roast,
rolled and boned
½ cup flour
4 tbsp Herb Gathering Leaf
Rosemary, minced
2 tbsp dry mustard
2 tbsp Andy's Seasoning Salt
2 tsp seasoned pepper

- Preheat oven to 350 degrees.
- Wipe roast with wet paper towel, leaving surface very moist.

- Combine flour and seasonings in a small bowl. Sprinkle evenly over moist surface of meat, patting on firmly.
- Place roast, fat side up, on rack in shallow roasting pan. Insert meat thermometer into roast so bulb reaches the center of the roast.
- Roast 3 hours or until thermometer registers 140-rare or 160-medium.
- Remove meat from oven; place on a heated serving platter. Cover loosely with foil and let stand 20 minutes before slicing.

*Missouri ranks second
in the nation
in the number
of farms,
cattle farms
and beef cows.*

Steak Round-Up

2 lb beef round steak
salt and pepper to taste
¾ cup Ott's Barbecue Sauce
1 tsp Aunt Joan's Ozark
Country Mustard
4½ oz Kraft® Processed
Swiss Cheese
2-6 toothpicks

- Lay steak out flat and season with salt and pepper.
- Spread with mustard, then with barbecue sauce.
- Arrange cheese slices to cover meat and then roll up (like a jelly roll).
- Secure with toothpicks and place in glass casserole dish.
- Cover and bake at 325 degrees for 60-90 minutes, until tender.
- Serves 8.

Saltimbocca alla Romana

12 small veal scallops,
(approximately 2 lbs),
pounded very thin
1 tsp of sage
4 tbsp butter
6 thin slices Volpi Prosciutto,
cut in half crosswise
½ cup Stone Hill Blush
Vidal Wine
1½ tsp ground sage
salt and pepper to taste

- Sprinkle veal slices with sage on both sides.
- Melt the butter in large skillet, add the veal slices and cook quickly over high heat for about 1 minute.
- Have the prosciutto slices ready and as the veal slices are being turned over, top them with prosciutto and cook for about 1 more minute.
- Carefully remove the veal from the pan, arrange on serving platter and keep warm.
- Add the wine, salt and pepper to the liquid in the pan. Reduce heat for a few seconds and then pour sauce over the veal and serve immediately.

William Becknell, a Missouri trader, followed the Santa Fe Trail as it snaked its way southwest from Missouri.

He learned that the Mexicans, newly independent from Spain and possessors of land crossed by the trail, were eager to re-initiate trade with the United States. Becknell rushed to develop a fur trade business in 1824 as business boomed along the trail, lasting continuously for two decades. The bountiful commercial activity was fueled in part by Mexican silver coming in and propping up Missouri's economy.

The Santa Fe Trail led from the town of Independence, which rose to prominence as "civilization's last outpost" for western-bound settlers. The village was a far cry from the way it looked when Lewis and Clark described Independence as "full of wild apples, deer, and bears."

Veal Cutlets Parmesan

¾ lb veal scallopine
or
4 chicken breast halves,
boneless, skinless,
(pounded to ¼" thick)
2 eggs, lightly beaten
¾ cup Italian style bread crumbs
6 tbsp Parmesan cheese,
divided usage
6 tbsp Hollywood Safflower Oil,
divided usage
1 (8 oz) can Progresso
Tomato Sauce
8 oz Mozzarella cheese, sliced

- Preheat oven to 350 degrees.
- Dip veal in egg, then in bread crumbs mixed with 4 tbsp of the Parmesan cheese.
- Refrigerate veal for 30 minutes or freeze for 5 minutes.
- In a large skillet, brown half of the veal in 3 tbsp hot oil, about 2 minutes on each side.
- Remove from skillet and repeat with remaining veal and oil.
- Place veal in a 13"x9"x2" baking dish.
- Pour tomato sauce over veal; top with mozzarella cheese and remaining Parmesan cheese.
- Bake until hot and bubbly, about 15 minutes.
- Broil for a few minutes to brown.
- Serves 4.

Bar-B-Qued Ham Steak with Sweet Mustard

hickory smoked boneless ham

- Slice ham into ¾" steaks. Score edge to keep slices from cupping. Grill 5 minutes, turn, spread with sweet mustard and grill another 5 minutes.

Home-Made Sweet Mustard:
1 cup Passport Seasonings Vinegar
3 oz dry mustard
2 eggs, slightly beaten
1 cup sugar
Pinch salt

- Combine vinegar and mustard, let stand overnight.
- Mix remaining ingredients, stirring to dissolve sugar.
- Add vinegar mixture; bring to boil; boil until mixture coats spoon 5-10 minutes.
- Keeps well in refrigerator.

Baked Bone-In Mild Ham with Bourbon Glaze

1 (14-16 lb) Alewel's Smoked Bone-In Mild Cured Ham
¾ cup bourbon
2 cups brown sugar
1 tbsp dry mustard
¾ cup whole cloves

- Place ham fat side up on rack in uncovered roasting pan.
- Bake in a 325 degree oven 16-18 minutes per pound.
- Last 30 minutes of baking remove ham, score fat in diamond shapes.
- Set oven to 450 degrees, brush ham on all sides with ½ cup of bourbon.
- Combine sugar and mustard and ¼ cup of bourbon.
- Pat mixture firmly into the scored fat. Stud fat with whole cloves.
- Baste lightly with drippings from pan and bake for 15-20 minutes - until sugar has formed brilliant glaze.

The early French explorers left their mark throughout Missouri in tha names they gave their rivers, towns, and special sites. Anglicized names based on meaning or corrupted pronunciation now replace many of the lilting French names.

In east central Missouri, for example, "Quiver River" had its origins in the French Creole designation "Riviere Au Cuivre" or "Copper River." It empties near Old Monroe into the Mississippi. Near Booneville, the "Lamine River" came from "Riviere de la Mine" or "River of Lead," near which were lead ore deposits. In a steep valley between Mineola and Danville is the "Otter River" a direct translation from the French "Loutre" River.

Quiche Lorraine

1 Pet-Ritz Regular Pie Crust Shell, thawed
6 slices Farmland Bacon, fried crisp and crumbled
1 (4 oz) can sliced mushrooms, drained
1 cup (4 oz) Swiss cheese, shredded
½ cup onion, diced
1 tbsp all-purpose flour
½ tsp salt
¼ tsp garlic powder
2 eggs
1 small (5 oz) can Pet Evaporated Milk

- Preheat oven and cookie sheet to 450 degrees.
- Prick bottom and sides of pie crust shell with fork. Partially bake pie crust on cookie sheet 5 minutes. Cool.
- Reduce oven temperature to 325 degrees.
- In bowl, combine bacon, mushrooms, cheese, onions, flour, salt, and garlic powder. Mix until well blended. Spoon into pie crust.
- Beat together eggs and evaporated milk. Slowly pour over bacon mixture.
- Bake on preheated cookie sheet 1 hour until it is slightly puffed and knife inserted near center comes out clean.
- Cool 15 minutes before serving.
- Serves 6.

For more than 30 years, Farmland Foods has been a quality name in the pork industry, producing hickory-smoked bacon, hams, sausage, and other pork products. It was in 1959 that Farmland Industries, then known as Consumers Cooperative Association (CCA), purchased the Crawford County Packing Company in Denison, Iowa. This purchase by CCA was the basis for the company known today as Farmland Foods.

Farmland products are marketed under the brand names Farmland and Maple River. An industry innovator, Farmland has introduced a lower-salt line of bacon, ham and sausage, and lower fat, lower salt hot dogs and lunch meats for the health-conscious consumer. Slim-line fresh pork products are custom cut to be leaner, juicier and more tender.

Today, Farmland Foods ranks 24th among all meat packers and 19th among the top 50 food companies. But size alone has never been the key to success. Farmland Foods is a company of people dedicated to providing products that stand for quality and exceptional value.

Tim Daugherty, vice president of management information services for Farmland Industries, states, "As a member of 4-H, I learned that leaders weren't extraordinary individuals. They were simply common people who harnessed their abilities, accepted responsibility, and made things happen."

Farmland makes good things happen for Missouri.

Easy Barbeque Meat Balls

1 lb Farmland Sausage
1 lb ground beef
1 env dry onion soup mix
1 egg
1 cup barbeque sauce

- Combine sausage, beef, soup mix and egg.
- Mix thoroughly and shape into 1″ meatballs.
- Broil 4″ from source of heat until browned.
- Put in slow cooker and pour in barbeque sauce.
- Set temperature to low and cook 4-5 hours.
- Serves 8.

Breakfast Pizza

1 pkg crescent rolls
1 lb Farmland Sausage
1 cup Mr. Dell's Frozen Hash
Brown Potatoes
1 cup Cheddar cheese, shredded
5 eggs
¼ cup Fairmont Milk
1 tbsp Mid-America Farms
Sour Cream
½ tsp salt
⅛ tsp pepper
2 tbsp Parmesan cheese

- Unroll each crescent and place with points together in the center of a pizza pan.
- Push and press until the edges are together to cover the bottom of the pan.
- Pinch the outside edges into a rim.
- Brown sausage and drain.
- Put the drained sausage over the crescent roll crust.
- Put frozen potatoes and cheese on top of sausage.
- Mix eggs, milk, sour cream, salt and pepper and pour over the sausage, potatoes and cheese.
- Sprinkle Parmesan cheese on top.
- Bake in 375 degree oven for 25-30 minutes.
- Serves 6-8.

Mexican Meat Loaf

1 egg, beaten
½ cup tomato sauce
1 (4 oz) can Old El Paso
Chopped Green Chilies, drained
1 (4 oz) can chopped mushrooms, drained
⅓ cup Old El Paso Nachips
Tortilla Chips, finely crushed
1 tsp salt
1 tsp chili powder
dash of black pepper
1½ lbs lean ground beef
¾ cup (3 oz) Monterey Jack
cheese, shredded

- Preheat oven to 400 degrees.
- In a large bowl, combine first 8 ingredients.
- Add meat and mix well.
- Spoon meat mixture into a lightly greased 1-qt loaf pan.
- Bake for 40 minutes.
- Sprinkle cheese on top and return to oven until cheese is melted.
- Serves 6.

Petrofsky's Bakery Products Inc., a 50-year-old St. Louis-based firm, thanks the popularity of bagels for its worldwide status.

Developed through the years from an old family recipe, Petrofsky's fresh bake bagels are mixed, blended, kneaded, formed, boiled and frozen according to a patented process.

Health-conscious consumers find the delicious bagels contain no cholesterol and are very low in fat. They are easy to eat, make perfect sandwiches, and are available in a variety of flavors.

But bagels are not all Petrofsky's offers. A complete line of fresh baked breads with an old world look and taste are Petrofsky's specialties. Pumpernickel, rye, sourdough or egg challa are baked rolled, round or braided, and have a naturally crispy crust. Petrofsky's breads have an authentic, European hearth-baked appearance. A new line of Hearth Breads, from recipes handed down through family archives, offer variety, delicious taste, and irresistible fresh-baked appeal.

Scotch Eggs

4 hard-cooked eggs
¼ lb Farmland Roll Sausage
4 Petrofsky's Bagels, made into bread crumbs
salt to taste
⅛ tsp ground sage
2 eggs, beaten
4 Petrofsky's Bagels, sliced and toasted

- Cover each hard-cooked egg with 1 oz of pork sausage.
- Mix bread crumbs with salt and ground sage.
- Dip sausage-coated egg into beaten raw egg and roll into bagel crumb mixture.
- Fry 5-6 minutes in saucepan turning occasionally.
- Serve hot or cold with bagels.
- Serves 4.

The Wilson Foods Corporation, located in Marshall, Missouri, is a modern and efficient pork slaughtering and processing facility whose products are ultimately distributed throughout the United States and in several foreign countries.

As an active partner in the business community, the facility employs more than 700 people and purchases over a million hogs per year, the majority coming from Missouri pork producers.

Wilson hams, marketed under the Wilson and Corn King labels, currently are the preferred brands in leading market areas throughout the United States. In addition to being number one in hams, Wilson also ranks among the top brands for bacon, sausage and cold cuts. Much of the raw material for these processed products is produced in Missouri. A pre-sliced, pre-packaged fresh pork product which is growing in popularity among retailers is produced exclusively at the Marshall facility and involves a patented process developed by Wilson for extending the shelf life.

Mustard Pork Chops

4 Wilson Pork Chops, ½" thick
4 oz Aunt Joan's Ozark Country Mustard
1 tsp salt
½ teaspoon pepper
2 oz soybean oil
1 (10¾ oz) can cream of chicken soup
4 oz water

- Spread both sides of pork chops generously with mustard.
- Into a large bowl put flour seasoned with salt and pepper.
- Cover pork chops with flour mix.
- Brown both sides of chops in frying pan with vegetable oil.
- Put browned chops into casserole, in a single layer.
- Pour off oil from frying pan, add cream of chicken soup plus water into the pan.
- When heated, pour over chops and bake at 350 degrees oven for 1 hour.
- Serves 4.

Missouri Spare Ribs

3 lbs Wilson Pork Spare Ribs
1 cup honey
1 (18 oz) bottle Ott's
Barbecue Sauce
seasoning salt or garlic salt,
to taste

- Boil ribs about 45 minutes in a small amount of water.
- Drain and save broth.
- Put ribs in roaster.
- Pour honey and barbeque sauce over ribs, and refrigerate overnight.
- Next day either bake in 375 degree oven, basting with broth, for 1 hour
  or
- Cook on grill, basting from time to time with the broth.
- Serves 4.

John H. Walker was a Missourian, and he wanted to stay one. He purchased a plantation in the southeasternmost part of the state where the land dips down into Arkansas. But, he soon found out he was no longer living in his beloved state.

This area, known as the bootheel of Missouri, was, in Walker's time, a swampy, overgrown area whose magnolia, gum and cypress trees loomed over snake-infested marshes. Not until Europeans and Americans involved in the fur trade began to frequent this mid-region of the Mississippi did anyone think of settling here.

Walker, though, bullheaded as he was, campaigned to have the land south of the thirty-sixth parallel between the St. Francis and Mississippi Rivers included in Missouri's state boundary. It was through his efforts that the bootheel now belongs to Missouri.

Stuffed Pork Chops with Pan Gravy

5 tbsp butter, divided
¼ cup minced onion
¼ cup minced celery
3 fresh mushrooms, minced
1 garlic clove, peeled and
mashed
½ tsp dried thyme
¼ tsp dried rosemary
½ cup fine dry bread crumbs
(made from Nancy Anne Roma
Italian Bread)
salt to taste
pepper to taste
6 pork loin butterfly chops
¼ cup light cream
pan gravy (optional)

- Melt 3 tbsp butter in a small saucepan over moderate heat.
- Add onion, celery, mushrooms, garlic, thyme and rosemary. Cook, stirring often until vegetables are tender.

- Remove saucepan from heat and stir in bread crumbs, salt and pepper; set mixture aside.
- Top each open chop with stuffing, dividing mixture evenly among the 6 chops. Fold each chop around filling, tie with kitchen string.
- Melt 2 tbsp butter in a large skillet and brown chops well on each side, 8-10 minutes.
- Put chops in an ungreased, shallow baking dish.
- Pour cream over chops and sprinkle with salt and pepper. Cover dish with aluminum foil and set in a preheated 350 degrees oven.
- Bake 1-1¼ hours. Remove string.
- Serve chops with pan gravy, if desired.
- Serves 6.

Pan Gravy:

2 tbsp butter
¼ cup all-purpose flour
2 cups liquid made from a
combination of drippings from
dish in which chops cooked and
beef broth, cream or milk
salt to taste
pepper to taste

- Add butter to skillet in which you browned chops, and set over medium heat.
- When butter melts, stir in flour. Cook, stirring constantly, 1 minute.
- Slowly add liquid and cook, stirring constantly, until mixture thickens, 3-5 minutes.
- Season with salt and pepper.

Several structures housed Jasper County records before the present stately courthouse was built in 1894 at a cost of $100,000. When Jasper County was organized in 1841, George Hamback's log cabin home was used for official business. A year later a one-room building was erected on the north side of the town square, and this served as the courthouse for 12 years.

A two-story brick building was completed in 1854 in the middle of the square, and stood until the Battle of Carthage in 1861, when it was severely damaged by heavy artillery. A short time later, it was completely destroyed by fire.

County court sessions were suspended during the Civil War, returning in October of 1865 to meet in the old Cave Spring School. In 1895, after a long and trying process of construction, the county government moved into the present magnificent structure.

Fifteen thousand citizens celebrated the laying of its cornerstone with a parade and $600 worth of fireworks.

On view today inside the ornate marble building is a mural that depicts 150 years of local history. Its creator, Lowell Davis, is a Carthage native and one of America's foremost nature artists.

Davis asked permission to paint a mural and was turned down by the county court. His dream was realized 20 years later when Soroptimist International Club of Carthage commissioned him to paint a mural as the club's Bicentennial gift to the city. Entitled "Forged in Fire," the mural was completed in 1976.

The majestic Jasper County Courthouse was officially placed on the national register of historic places in 1973.

The majestic Jasper County Courthouse,
on the National Register
of Historic Places,
is the showcase of Carthage,
the home of Ott Food Products.

Carthage Pork Steaks

6 large pork steaks
1 bag hickory chips
water, as needed

Lizzie Sauce:
3 cups Ott's Barbeque Sauce
½ cup clover honey
¼ cup soy sauce
¼ cup Ott's Famous Dressing
¼ cup parsley flakes
½ tsp ground cinnamon
½ tsp ground pepper
pinch of celery seed
pinch of nutmeg
¼ cup Peach Basket Schnapps or
Cherry Sloe Gin (optional)

- Combine all sauce ingredients in a blender and blend for 2 minutes.
- Light charcoal briquets in grill.
- Soak hickory chips in pan with water.
- Add handful of chips to charcoal. Let fire and chips smoke about 15-20 minues.
- Baste the pork steaks with the Lizzie Sauce and place on the back of the grill rack.
- Smoke the pork steaks, turning every 45 minutes, and basting with the sauce to keep steaks from drying out.
- Smoke approximately 4-5 hours, adding handful of chips every 45 minutes.
- Serves 6.

Schnitzel

1 egg
1 tbsp milk
1 cup plain bread crumbs
¼ cup soybean oil
4 thin (½" thick) Wilson
Boneless Pork Steaks

- In medium bowl, beat together egg and milk.
- On a flat dish, spread bread crumbs.
- Dip each pork steak in egg and milk, then coat with bread crumbs.
- Fry pork steaks in oil over medium heat until bread crumbs are browned and meat is white, about 2 minutes on each side.
- Serves 4.

Orange-Pecan Glazed Pork Roast

½ cup onion, chopped
⅛ tsp instant garlic, minced
2 tbsp soybean oil
¼ cup pecans, chopped
½ cup orange marmalade
¼ tsp cinnamon
2 lb Wilson Boneless Pork Roast

- Saute onion and garlic in oil.
- Add remaining ingredients, except pork roast. Heat.
- Pour over roast. Insert meat thermometer into center of roast.
- Bake meat in 325 degree oven to internal temperature of 170 degrees (about 40-45 minutes per pound).
- Remove from oven and let stand 15 minutes before carving.
- Serves 4-6.

Stuffed Roast Pork Loin

5 lb Wilson's Boneless Pork Loin
2 lb Shiitake mushrooms
2 oz pine nuts
1 lb spinach leaves
2 cups port wine
salt and pepper to taste
1 egg, beaten
1 qt pork demi or stock

- Saute mushrooms, spinach and pine nuts in ¼ cup wine. Add salt and pepper, to taste.
- Mix mushroom mixture and egg.
- Insert a long, thin knife into the loin.
- Cut a 1″ slit through loin, stuff with spinach and mushroom mixture. Insert meat thermometer into center of loin.
- Bake at 350 degrees for 1 hour, 20 minutes, to internal temperature of 170 degrees.
- Remove from oven and let sit for 15 minutes.
- Reduce pork demi or stock until syrupy.
- Flame the rest of the wine and pour into demi.
- Add salt and pepper to taste.
- Serve with garnish of whole Shiitake mushrooms and watercress.
- Serves 6-8.

The wine industry had its beginning in 1823 when the Jesuits of St. Stanislaus first produced sacramental wine for their Florissant parish.

However, it wasn't until German settlers trekked into Missouri that grapes began to grow widespread across the countryside.

During the War Between the States, General Sterling Price's Confederates raided Hermann just for the privilege of consuming all the wine in George Husmann's cellar.

And by the end of the 19th century, Missouri ranked second in the nation in wine production, proudly boasting a hundred wineries. At the World's Fair in 1904, Augusta wines even took four of the five medals awarded.

Today, the Missouri wine country has more than 30 wineries, most of them open for tours, and the fields around Cuba, St. James and Rolla are thick with vineyards.

For Missouri's wine country, every year is a vintage year.

Hasenpfeffer

2 cups water
¼ cup Stone Hill Chancellor or Hermanns Berger Red Wine
½ cup vinegar
3 tbsp sugar
1 tsp salt
½ tsp whole cloves
½ tsp whole black pepper
1 bay leaf
1 rabbit, cut up for frying
3 tbsp butter
1 medium onion, chopped
1½ tbsp flour
3 tbsp water
½ cup Mid-America Farms Sour Cream

- Mix together first 8 ingredients and heat to boiling point. Cool.
- Put rabbit in glass bowl and cover with wine mixture. Cover; refrigerate overnight.
- Remove rabbit and brown in hot butter. Add onion.
- Strain wine mixture and add ½ cup to browned rabbit. Cover; simmer 1 hour.
- Make paste of flour and water; stir into rabbit liquid.
- Boil 2 minutes, stir in sour cream; heat to boiling.
- Serve at once.
- Serves 4.

Perched dramatically on a hilltop near Hermann, Missouri, is Stone Hill Winery. In 1836, German settlers chose these hills along the Missouri River which resembled their beloved Rhineland, famous for some of the world's finest white wines. In 1847, Stone Hill began making wine, growing to become the third largest winery in the world by the turn of the century.

In 1920, when Prohibition devastated the wine industry in Missouri, Stone Hill survived by using its enormous cellars to grow mushrooms. These arched cellars buried in the hill slopes, are the largest series of cellars in America.

Restored and renovated, Stone Hill began producing wine again in 1965, winning regional, national and international awards for Catawba, Vidal, Nillard-Noir, Norton, Seyval and Vignoles. Wine lovers delight in Stone Hill's Missouri Riesling, available only in Missouri. Recent entries have been the Blush, Spumante Blush and Golden Spumante, taking their place alongside Stone Hill's celebrated champagne.

At the 1990 Florida State Fair, 61 wineries were chosen medal-winners from over 500 entries. Stone Hill won more than twice as many medals as any other winery.

The Stone Hill Winery has been declared a National Historic District, and is open year-round to the public.

Marinated Leg of Lamb Filet

6 Missouri Leg of Lamb Filets, cut ½" thick
1 clove garlic, minced
½ tsp ground pepper
¼ tsp dried thyme
¼ tsp dried marjoram
¼ tsp dried oregano
1 tsp Worcestershire sauce
¼ cup olive oil
1 cup Stone Hill Chancellor or Hermann's Berger Wine
1 medium onion, sliced

- Arrange lamb in baking dish.
- Combine all ingredients.
- Pour over lamb and marinate in refrigerator for several hours or overnight.
- Remove from marinade.
- Broil 4 inches from heat for 8-10 minutes; turn; broil 8 minutes.
- Serves 6.

Vineyard Leg of Lamb

*5-6 lb leg of lamb, trimmed of
excess fat and fell removed
2 medium-sized garlic cloves,
peeled and cut length-wise
1 cup brandy
1 tsp ground cumin
1½ tbsp salt
2 tsp freshly ground black pepper
¼ cup dry sherry
¼ cup Stone Hill Vidal Dry
White Wine
sprigs of watercress for garnish*

- With sharp knife, cut a dozen 1"-deep slits on surface of the lamb; insert sliver of garlic into each slit.
- Cut a double thickness of cheesecloth; drench thoroughly with ½ cup brandy.
- Wrap lamb in cheesecloth and cover tightly with plastic wrap. Let set at room temperature for 1 hours.
- Preheat the oven to 450 degrees.
- Mix the cumin, salt and pepper in a bowl: combine sherry and wine in another bowl.
- Unwrap lamb; place fat side up in roasting pan.
- Press cumin mixture into surface of lamb. Insert meat thermometer 2" into the thickest part of the leg.
- Roast in middle of oven 20 minutes.
- Reduce heat to 350 degrees. Baste with tbsp of wine mixture. Continue to roast 40-60 minutes longer, basting 2-3 times with remaining wine mixture. Thermometer will register 150 degrees when well done.
- Transfer lamb to heated platter. Let rest 15 minutes for easier carving.
- Just before serving, warm remaining ½ cup of brandy in saucepan. Ignite the brandy and pour it flaming over the lamb.
- Garnish the platter with sprigs of watercress and serve.
- Serves 6-8.

When we think of trends and trend-setting places, we think of Los Angeles and New York, not Carthage, Missouri. But some analysts now believe the Midwest is where trends are beginning.

"When it comes to food, the coasts are not the only ones on the cutting edge." says Jack Crede, co-owner of Ott Food Products in Carthage, maker of Ott's Famous Dressing.

Crede says cooks are going back to the basics and straying away from complicated dishes. He continues, "We have been doing it this way for years, now the rest of the country is starting to catch up."

"One reason for all this change is people are staying at home more everywhere, and not just here in the Midwest," affirms Crede's partner, Roy Moore. "Instead of going out for a quick bite, people stay at home and prepare the evening meal, from salad to dessert. It's become a pleasant, comforting pastime, rather than a chore."

Crede adds, "There is a resurgence of traditional family values. People want sit-down meals the whole family can enjoy. Quality time is rare these days, and the family meal is a great time to be together."

Recent studies indicate families are eating hearty meals like pot roast with carrots and potatoes, green beans, a basket of fresh-baked bread, a big salad and pie for dessert. Other meals may include meat loaf, barbecue, fried chicken, pork chops, or brisket served with simply prepared vegetables like corn, peas and mashed potatoes with gravy. Others opt for "nouvelle cuisine," as long as it is quick and easy to prepare.

"Comfort foods remind us of our childhood when our mothers prepared bountiful meals for their families," says Jack.

"The types of meals many of us grew up on are staging a comeback. Comfort food is not new, though," he adds. "It has been around for a long time and has been the source of many food trends."

The Ott's folks say much of this food has its roots in the Midwest where it is plucked fresh from the farms, fields and lakes of the Heartland.

"Throughout the years, traditions and recipes have been handed down from generation to generation," relates Roy.

"A few changes and improvements were made along the way, but the dishes are as wholesome as ever. We're finding that many people use salad dressings to enhance the flavor of several foods, not only salads. These cooks are aware of their families' nutritional needs, so they delete the fat, sugar and salt from their old recipes and add dressing to replace these unhealthful additives with the tasty, healthful alternative."

"Midwestern cuisine's emphasis on freshness and simplicity is right on track with America's return to more traditional values and the concern for better health," says Roy Moore of Ott's. "With the decline in the amount of free time of working Americans, this combination fits the profile for the 1990s. Ott's has served this need for over 40 years."

Herb Cheese Chicken Florentine

4 chicken breast halves, boned and skinned
8 oz garlic herb cream cheese
1 bunch fresh spinach
½ cup Ott's Ozark Maid Buttermilk Dressing
1 cup bread crumbs
¼ cup Parmesan cheese

- Spray 11"x13" baking pan with non-stick vegetable oil.
- Place chicken breast between two sheets of wax paper and pound to flatten.
- Wash spinach and remove stems.
- Steam in microwave for 2 minutes. Drain well.
- Cover each chicken breast with drained spinach leaves.
- Portion 2 oz herb cheese on spinach and rollup. Secure with toothpick if necessary.
- Dip into Ott's Ozark Maid Buttermilk Dressing and roll in bread crumbs mixed with Parmesan cheese.
- Bake in 350 degree oven 45 minutes.
- Serves 4.

Lemon-Honey Chicken

3 lbs Hudson Chicken, skinned
and cut in serving pieces
1 tbsp soybean oil
¼ cup Gibbons Creme Honey
½ cup lemon juice
2 tbsp soy sauce
1 tsp lemon peel, grated
1 tsp paprika
¼ tsp nutmeg

- Lay chicken in baking pan.
- Combine remaining ingredients to make sauce.
- Pour sauce over chicken, turning pieces to coat.
- Bake uncovered in 350 degree oven for 1 hour, or until done, turning and basting once.
- Serves 4.

Mustard Chicken

3 lbs Hudson Chicken
Breasts, skinned
½ cup Aunt Joan's Ozark
Country Mustard
2 eggs, beaten
2½ cups fresh bread crumbs
1 tbsp paprika
1 tsp tarragon
1 tsp ground pepper
3 tbsp butter
3 tbsp Hollywood Safflower Oil
⅓ cup fresh lemon juice

- Brush chicken with mustard to coat. Cover and marinate for 30 minutes.
- Preheat the oven to 375 degrees. Beat eggs in a bowl. In a pie pan or shallow dish, combine the bread crumbs with the paprika, tarragon and pepper.
- Dip mustard-coated chicken pieces into the egg and roll in the crumb mixture to coat evenly, place in a shallow baking dish large enough to hold the chicken in a single layer.
- Melt butter in the oil over low heat. Remove from heat and stir in the lemon juice.
- Spoon half of the lemon butter over the chicken pieces. Bake for 30 minutes.
- Spoon the remaining lemon butter over the chicken and bake 30 minutes. Let stand for 15 minutes before serving.
- Serves 6-8.

Four-H makes a difference in the lives of thousands of youths. Testimony to this comes from the members themselves:

As one says, "I was not interested in anything much until I got involved with 4-H, and then my life seemed to change. I would probably have dropped out of school like my brothers did. Instead of giving up, I discovered that someone besides my parents believed I could do better. I learned that if I wanted to do better, I needed to start believing in myself as well. I went from F's to D's to graduating with a 3.5 average. Plans to attend college this fall are on schedule."

Shiitake Chicken Breasts

8 Hudson Skinless, Boneless Chicken Breast Halves, pounded flat
flour, as needed
salt and pepper, to taste
⅓ cup oil
3 shallots, minced
1 lb fresh Shiitake mushrooms
¾ cup Pirtle's Weston Bend White Wine
1 cup chicken stock or canned broth
2 tbsp lemon juice
¾ cup creme fraiche or heavy cream

- Dredge the chicken breasts in flour. Sprinkle with salt and pepper.
- Heat oil in saute pan.
- Add minced shallots; stir-fry 2 minutes. Remove shallots from pan.

- Increase heat to high. Add chicken in batches; saute 1 minute per side. Remove from pan.
- Remove stems from the mushrooms; slice into slivers. Saute in pan until most of the liquid is evaporated. Transfer to a bowl.
- Add wine to saute pan; bring to boil. Boil 2-3 minutes until wine reduces to a rich amber glaze.
- Return shallots to saute pan, add the chicken stock and lemon juice. Boil, stirring constantly, 3-4 minutes.
- Stir in the creme fraiche and boil about 2 minutes until reduced by half.
- Reduce heat to low, add chicken and mushrooms and heat through, spooning over sauce about 2 minutes.
- Serves 8.

Concord Chicken a la Meramec

2 whole Hudson's Chickens
(about 2 lb fryers)
2 eggs
6 shredded wheat biscuits
1 cup Central Dairy Milk
1 cup seeded concord grapes
¼ cup Meramec Vineyards
Concord Grape Juice
¼ tsp coriander seeds, crushed
¼ tsp mace
¼ tsp white pepper
¼ cinnamon
1 tsp salt

- Preheat oven to 375 degrees.
- Wash chickens and pat dry with paper towels.
- Mix all the ingredients together and stuff into the chickens.
- Skewer chickens to help keep stuffing inside birds. Place on a rack in an oven proof dish and bake for 50-60 minutes.
- Baste with pan drippings to promote even browning. Serves 4.
- Chicken can also be grilled over hot coals in a kettle style bar-b-que grill for about the same amount of time.

Bagels A La Queen

2 Petrofsky's Sprouted Wheat
Bagels
¼ cup fresh or canned
mushrooms, sliced
¼ cup green peppers, diced
1½ cups prepared white sauce
¼ cup Stone Hill White Wine
1 cup Hudson's Chicken, cooked
and diced

- Slice bagel in half and toast.
- Saute mushrooms and green peppers in butter or non-stick spray.
- In sauce pan, make your favorite white sauce.
- To white sauce, stir in mushrooms, green peppers, white wine and chicken. When sauce thickens, pour over bagel halves.
- Serves 2.

Hudson Foods, founded in 1972 by James T. "Red" Hudson, is the fourth largest publicly traded poultry company in the U.S. Hudson chicken, turkey, egg and processed meat products are marketed to retail supermarket chains, fast food chains, restaurants, schools, foodservice distributors, convenience stores and prepared food companies.

Changing lifestyles have spurred consumer demand for nutritional and convenient foods that are quickly and easily prepared. Answering this demand, Hudson processes a wide range of food products tailored specifially to meet the needs of various markets.

The Hudson Broiler division cuts, packages and labels a diverse line of chicken for supermarkets throughout the country. The Hudson "Flavor Fresh® " label is found on more than 50 items of chill-pack chicken. Hudson supplies fresh whole and pre-cut chicken and numerous processed items to food-service operators.

From Hudson's Turkey Division comes a variety of turkey products, such as turkey sausage, turkey ham, boneless breasts, ground turkey and boneless breast roasts. These products are distributed to supermarkets, food services and the military, and custom meats are prepared for food processors.

Broiler processing plants in Alabama, Arkansas, Indiana, Maryland and Missouri have the capacity to produce approximtely 700 million pounds of dressed chicken annually. Each plant has a fully equipped quality assurance laboratory where all products are tested to meet or exceed U.S.D.A. regulations for food safety and quality.

At Springfield, Missouri, Hudson's turkey processssing facility has an annual capacity of 100 million pounds of dressed turkey. A new, second facility offers complete further processing, including cooking of a substantial amount of value-added turkey products.

Growth-oriented Hudson's most recent acquisitions include Pierre Frozen Foods, Inc. and the meat products division of Land O'Lakes, Inc., which includes Land O'Lakes Turkey and Schweigert Meat Products.

Missouri's Prize Grilled Turkey Steaks

½ cup Hermannoff Seyval Blanc Wine
¼ cup soy sauce
1 tbsp vegetable oil
1 clove garlic, mashed, or
¼ teaspoon garlic powder
1 lb Hudson Turkey Breast Steaks, ¾-1" thick

- Combine wine, soy sauce, oil and garlic in glass dish.
- Add turkey steaks, turning to coat both sides.
- Cover and marinate in refrigerator at least 2 hours.
- Turn steaks in marinade several times.
- Grill drained turkey steaks over medium hot coals 5-7 minutes per side, basting with marinade a couple of times.
- Serves 3-4.

Garden Sauteed Turkey Steaks

2-3 tbsp butter or margarine
¼ cup flour
½ tsp fresh ground pepper
½ tsp garlic powder
½ tsp paprika
½ tsp salt
6 Hudson Turkey Breast Steaks, ½" thick
1 cup cherry tomatoes
2 cups broccoli flowerettes
1 cup zucchini, sliced
½ tsp basil or marjoram

- Melt 2 tbsp butter or margarine.
- Combine flour, pepper, garlic powder, paprika and salt.
- Dredge steaks in seasoned flour mixture and saute about 4-5 minutes per side, until nicely browned and done.
- Remove to serving platter and keep warm.
- Add remaining butter to skillet and stir fry vegetables about 5 minutes to desired doneness.
- Sprinkle on basil and marjoram and toss.
- Arrange over or around turkey steaks on platter.
- Serves 6.

The War Between the States left a bloody trail across peaceful fields. Only Tennessee and Virginia, in fact, had more battles and skirmishes than did Missouri.

Armies dueled at Carthage, Lexington, Westport and Boonville. But the most important conflict erupted on Wilson's Creek near Springfield.

The battle lasted little more than 4 hours, yet it was one of the bloodiest of the war.

As one Union private wrote:

"On the edge of the meadow. . . was a low rail fence; the Rebels rallied under the shelter of it, and, as if by some inspiration or some immediate change of orders, they broke it down in places and started for our artillery. As they got nearer to us, their own artillery ceased firing, because it endangered them. When they got close the firing began on both sides. How long it lasted I do not know; it was probably 20 minutes. Every man was shooting as fast, on our side, as he could load, and yelling as loud as his breath would permit. Most were on the ground, some on one knee. The foe stopped advancing. We had paper cartridges, and in loading we had to bite off the end, and every man had a big quid of paper in his mouth, from which down his chin ran the dissolved gunpowder. The other side was yelling, and if any orders were given nobody heard them. Every man assumed the responsibility of doing as much shooting as he could."

The battle also had its moments of heroism.

An Iowa infantryman recalled:

" A flag was seen lying on the ground about 150 yards in front of us, but no one was ordered or cared to undertake to go and bring it in. In a few minutes a solitary horseman was seen coming toward us, as if to surrender, and the cry therefore rose from us, 'Don't shoot!" When within about 20 yards of that flag, the horseman spurred his horse, and, leaping from his saddle, picked the flag from the grass, and off he went with it a-flying. The flag bore the 'Lone Star' of Texas, and we didn't shoot at the horseman because we liked his nerve."

And the battle had its moments of grim humor.

A Union cavalry officer, trying to inspire his men, yelled, "Life ain't long enough for them to lick us in."

But he was wrong.

The day of battle came to end, with Union troops retreating from the fields of Wilson Creek. Yet, the Confederates were too tired to follow.

Both had suffered a terrible toll. The Federals lost 1,317 men. The Rebels reported 1,230 casualties.

The Rev. R. A. Austin of Carrollton, Missouri, a chaplain in General Slack's Division, would say: "It makes the heart sad to think of the hearts that have been lacerated with grief and the tears that are being shed; the ties that have been broken and the sufferings that have resulted from this bloody conflict. May a merciful God interpose and drive back the red cloud of war which hovers over us. May the Angel of Peace which has flapped her wings and left us, once more return to our beautiful and once happy country."

Gingered Turkey Stir-Fry

1 lb fresh Hudson Turkey Breast
4 tbsp soy sauce
½ cup pineapple juice
2 tbsp dry sherry
¼ tsp ginger
1 tbsp cornstarch
3 tbsp soybean oil
½ bunch fresh broccoli, separated into flowerettes, stems sliced
1 red bell pepper, cut into strips
½ bunch green onions, sliced ⅛"
thick on diagonal
1 clove garlic, minced
3 cups hot cooked rice

- Cut turkey breast diagonally into ⅛ inch thick slices.

- Combine soy sauce, pineapple juice, sherry, ginger and cornstarch in glass bowl.
- Stir in turkey slices. Marinate in refrigerator ½-1 hour.
- Heat oil in a large skillet or wok.
- Drain turkey; reserve marinade.
- Add turkey to skillet; cook until it loses pink color. Remove from skillet.
- Add broccoli, red pepper, green onion and garlic to skillet and stir-fry 3-5 minutes.
- Add reserved marinade, bring to a boil and simmer 1-2 minutes.
- Return turkey to skillet; heat through.
- Serve over hot cooked rice.
- Serves 4.

Turkey and Old Fashioned Country Corn Bread Dressing

1 (10-16 lb) Hudson Turkey
10 biscuits, (can use canned)
1 (6 oz) pkg yellow corn bread mix, prepared
1 large loaf Butternut White or Whole Wheat Bread
2 eggs
1½ cup onion, chopped
2 cups celery, chopped
1 cup celery tops, chopped
1 tbsp sage, (or more to taste)
1 tbsp poultry seasoning
2 cups water
1 cup turkey drippings
salt and pepper to taste

- Roast turkey according to directions on package. Save the turkey drippings.
- Bake the biscuits and corn bread, and toast the loaf of bread. Then break all toasted and baked breads into small pieces and put them into a big pot and set aside.
- Put all remaining ingredients, except eggs, in a big saucepan. Let boil 10 minutes or until the celery and onions are tender.
- Pour this mixture over the broken bread and toss. If not as moist as you like, add turkey broth or water.
- Add the eggs and mix lightly again. (It is not necessary to beat the eggs.)
- Place the dressing on a greased or foil-lined cookie sheet, and cook at 350 degrees for at least 30 minutes. If you like it extremely moist, pile the dressing high. If you want a drier dressing, spread it about 2″ thick on the cookie sheet.
- Serves 12.

The Pirtle Winery in Weston has developed a honey wine, more commonly called mead.

It was the original wine in history, enjoyed even before grapes were cultivated.

The Norsemen and Vikings were well known for drinking mead. But when the English were introduced to honey wine, they called it a "Love Potion," which is how the word honeymoon originated.

Mead is a perfect after dinner wine, especially with fruit and cheese.

Coquilles St. Jacque Mornay

1 cup Pirtle's Weston Bend White Wine
1½ cup water
½ tsp salt
⅛ tsp pepper
1 tbsp onion, minced
2 lbs fresh sea scallops, sliced
½ lb fresh mushrooms, sliced
1 cup milk
2 tbsp butter
3 tbsp flour
½ cup Swiss cheese, shredded
2 tbsp Parmesan cheese
¼ cup heavy cream, whipped
¼ cup butter, melted
3 tbsp fresh parsley, chopped

- Combine wine, water, salt, pepper and onion in saucepan; simmer for 5 minutes.
- Add scallops and mushrooms; cover and simmer 5 minutes.
- Remove from pan and reserve.
- Cook fish stock remaining until it is reduced to 1 cup. Heat milk just to boiling.
- Melt butter , stir in flour and cook over low heat, stirring constantly for 3 minutes.
- Remove from heat.
- Stir in fish stock and milk rapidly with a wooden spoon or a wire whisk.
- Cook over low heat, stirring constantly until bubbly. Cook 1 minute longer.
- Stir in ¼ cup Swiss cheese and the Parmesan cheese.
- Remove and reserve ⅔ cup of sauce.
- Heat oven to 375 degrees.
- To remaining sauce, add scallops and mushrooms.
- Spoon mixture into 6 large buttered scallop shells or individual casseroles.
- Add cream to reserved sauce. Spread over scallop mixture.
- Sprinkle with remaining Swiss cheese.
- Drizzle the tops with butter.
- Bake until sauce bubbles and top is lightly brown.
- Sprinkle with parsley.
- Serves 6.

When the German settlers journeyed into Missouri in 1837, they nailed their homesteads to land that reminded them of their beloved Rhine Valley.

They called their new town Hermann and believed that it would forever be a city where the German culture could flourish, a city that would be "German in every particular."

Hermann still proudly upholds the traditions of its ancestors with a Maifest and an Octoberfest and a National Historic District that showcases the grand architectural heritage of more than a hundred buildings, all crafted before 1870. The town's beautifully restored homes range from Victorian mansions to cozy country cottages.

It is the last vestige from another century, an antique whose value increases with every passing year.

Aunt Nene's Shrimp Jambalaya

3 slices Farmland Bacon, diced
½ cup onion, chopped
½ celery, chopped
½ green pepper, chopped
½ tbsp garlic, minced
4 cups canned tomatoes with liquid
1 tsp chili powder
¼ cup Aunt Nene's Country-Style Chili Sauce
⅛ tsp cayenne pepper
¼ cup thyme, crumbled
2 lbs shrimp, cooked, peeled and deveined
¼ cup parsley, finely chopped
salt to taste
4 cups hot cooked rice

- Fry bacon and, when it is crisp, drain on paper towels and set aside.
- Over medium heat saute onion, celery and green pepper in the bacon fat.
- Add the garlic, tomatoes, chili powder, chili sauce, cayenne pepper and thyme.
- Lower heat and simmer 20 minutes.
- Add the shrimp, parsley and salt to the tomato sauce and cook for a few minutes until shrimp is hot.
- Mound the rice on a platter, spoon the shrimp and tomato sauce over it.
- Serves 8.

Ed Turner, of Chillicothe, was presented the 4-H Director's Award at the first 4-H Alumni Reunion in Columbia on September 16, 1989. He promptly remarked, "Mom caused it all," referring to his mother, Nellie Mable Turner.

Mrs. Turner has been recognized by the Missouri 4-H Foundation for her support of the program and for encouraging her family to participate in all aspects of 4-H.

Golden Fried Oysters

1 qt large oysters
¼ cup milk
2 eggs, beaten
1 cup flour
1½ cups Andy's Fish Breading
Oil for frying

- Drain oysters.
- Combine eggs and milk.
- Combine flour and fish breading.
- Roll oysters in flour mixture.
- Dip in milk and egg mixture, then again in flour mixture.
- Fry in very hot oil until golden brown.
- Serves 6.

Frog Legs with Fried Parsley

2 eggs, beaten
12 frog legs
½ cup lemon juice
1 teaspoon Andy's Seasoned Salt
1½ cups Andy's Fish Breading
¼ cup soybean oil
1 cup parsley, chopped
1 lemon, sliced

- Beat eggs in bowl; set aside.
- Scald frog legs for 4 minutes in boiling water, containing lemon juice and seasoned salt.
- Dip frog legs in egg and roll in breading.
- Drop into heated oil, fry until brown.
- Remove from oil, drain.
- Fry parsley in oil for 1 minute.
- Place frog legs on plate; garnish with fried parsley and fresh lemon slices.
- Serves 6.

In 1860, any male under age 18 who qualified with the following job requirements could become part of a brief yet very bold part of American history.

WANTED: Young, skinny, wiry fellows, not over 18.

Must be expert riders willing to risk death daily. Orphans preferred. Wages: $25 per week.

The company established in 1860 out of St. Joseph was called the Pony Express. Its mandate was to maintain communication lines from Missouri across the 1,982 miles to California as the only other routes used crossed southern territory. One of the dedicated young riders was Buffalo Bill Cody who once rode 300 miles without stopping. The Pony Express never lost a mail bag during its exciting history. It was the cross-country telegraph system which made the successful system obsolete.

Make-Ahead Crab Casserole

1 lb fresh lump crabmeat
3 green onions and tops, chopped
1 large lemon, juice
3 cups French bread, cut in 1" cubes
8 oz process cheese, grated
5 tbsp Daricraft Butter, melted
1¾ cups Fairmont Milk
3 eggs, beaten
½ tsp salt
3 drops hot pepper sauce
½ tsp dry mustard

- Toss crabmeat lightly with onions and lemon juice
- In buttered 1½ qt shallow casserole, arrange alternating layers of bread drizzled with melted butter and cheese-crab-onion mixture.
- Combine remaining ingredients. Pour over crab mixture, cover and refrigerate overnight.
- Remove from refrigerator 1 hour before baking.
- Bake uncovered at 350 degrees for 50-60 minutes or until puffed and golden.
- Serves 6-8.

The tough-talking, tabasco-tempered Harry S. Truman may have been the only Missourian elected President of the United States, but he was not the first Missourian to occupy the White House. That distinction belongs to Julia Dent of St. Louis, the wife of Ulysses S. Grant.

Orange Roughy-Three Ways

¾ cup buttermilk
¼ cup flour
½ tsp Andy's Seasoned Salt
2 lbs orange roughy filets
oil for frying or butter
1 stick Mid-America Farms Butter
¼ cup lemon juice
2 cups Andy's Fish Breading

(1) **For Frying:** Drop in hot oil until brown.

(2) **For Baking or Broiling:** Melt butter or margarine in sauce pan, add lemon juice.

• Prepare fish as for frying, then brush lightly lemon juice and butter mixture.

• Place on broiler rack, under medium flame until desired brown. Broil three inches from heat.

(3) **To Bake:** Place in shallow pan lightly sprayed with non-stick spray.

• Combine buttermilk, flour and seasoned salt.

• Wash fish, pat dry with paper towel, dip in buttermilk and flour batter, roll in breading.

• Brush with lemon juice and butter.

• Bake 10 to 15 minutes in 325 degree oven.

Baked Fish Filets

lemon juice
2 tbsp Worcestershire sauce
2 tbsp grainy mustard
1½ cups Hiland Sour Cream
2 lbs Party Steak Fish Filets

• Spoon seasoning over fish in shallow baking dish.

• Cover with sour cream and bake in a preheated 350 degree oven for 20 minutes or until flaky.

Missourians eat tastier beef, pork, fish and chicken thanks to Reuben Anderson and his Andy's Seasoning, Inc. Anderson experimented with many different ingredients in the basement of his home before producing his award-winning barbecue sauce in the fall of 1981.

With the growth in popularity of his spicy sauce, he branched out with Andy's Fish Breading two years later, quickly followed by the introduction of Chicken Breading and Seasoning Salt. In the summer of 1984, these products moved into the mainstream of major chain stores from his St. Louis store front operation.

By October of 1985, Andy's Seasoning began supplying 10,000 pounds of product per week to a prominent fast food chain, opening still another market.

Recently Rueben Anderson moved his company into a new $2.8 million dollar state-of-the art facility, capable of producing more than 80,000 pounds of product per day.

Anderson fondly remembers his experience as a 4-H member: "As a 4-H member, my project was with a little pig. I presented it at the fair and didn't win a ribbon, but what I remember most was the experience of getting the pig ready and showing it.

Hot & Spicy Salmon Cakes

1 can salmon and juices
½ cup Progresso Bread Crumbs
2 eggs
1 small onion
1 small green pepper
2 stalks celery, diced
¼ tsp Andy's Seasoned Salt
2 cups Andy's Chicken Breading, Hot & Spicy
Oil for frying

- Pour juice from salmon into bowl, add bread crumbs.
- Beat eggs. Fold into bread crumbs and salmon juice.
- Add onion, green pepper, celery and seasoned salt.
- Stir salmon into mixture.
- Use ice cream scoop to make balls, roll in breading.
- Flatten, fry in hot oil.
- Serves 4-6

While playing cards in the Old West, a carved piece of a buck's antler was placed in front of the person who was to deal the next hand. If the player did not want to deal, he picked up the piece and "passed the buck" on to the person beside him. This individual could choose to deal or simply "pass the buck" again to the next player. Over time, the expression evolved to signify the shirking of one's responsibilities.

When Missouri's Harry Truman was the thirty-third President, he adamantly refused to "pass the buck," and accepted total responsibility for his actions. On his desk was a plaque that read: "The buck stops here."

Marinated White Fish

⅓ bottle Mission Creek Dry Seyval Blanc Wine
4 white fish filets (orange roughy is preferred)
dillweed
garlic salt
½ stick Mid-America Farms Butter

- In shallow glass dish pour wine about 1/4″ deep.
- Lay in chilled fish filets.
- Dust exposed surface with dillweed and light garlic salt.
- Add small pats of butter.
- 20 minutes later, rotate filets. Dust exposed surface with dillweed and light garlic salt. Finish marinating for 20-30 minutes.
- Cook in microwave for 6 minutes until light and flaky.
- Serves 4.

Lemon Pepper Catfish

4 Country Fresh Catch Catfish
Filets
Andy's Seasoning Salt
lemon pepper
½ cup Mission Creek White Wine
⅓ cup pine nuts, slivered
fresh parsley, chopped
garnish of fresh parsley sprigs

- Wash catfish filets and pat dry with paper towels.
- Spray skillet with butter-flavored non-stick spray.
- Sprinkle filets with seasoning salt and lemon pepper.
- Lightly brown in skillet over medium heat, turning once.
- Pour wine over fish; reduce heat to simmer.
- Sprinkle with pine nuts and chopped parsley.
- Remove from heat after 10-15 minutes.
- Garnish with fresh parsley.
- Serves 4.

The Ozark mountain country lakes have long been a mecca for the nation's fishermen.

Lake Taneycomo has been recognized as the top producer of trout in the country, even nicknamed the nation's Trout Machine by *Sports Afield Magazine* simply because it yields 750,000 fish a year. Lay them all end to end, and you've got a stringer of fish 48 miles long. The fighting rainbows average twelve inches in length. The deep waters are also thick with black bass, smallmouths, Kentuckies and white bass. The lake record for a largemouth black bass is 10 pounds and 12 ounces.

However, Bull Shoals claims a majority of the state records. The largemouth record is 13 pounds, 14 ounces, while the biggest striper topped the scales at more than 47 pounds. A five-pound, four-ounce white bass tied the world record. And the lower lake has been known to hold some giant rainbows.

Table Rock has jetting points, countless coves, and miles and miles of tributaries where fishermen battle spotted bass, black bass, and lunker rainbow trouts.

Chinese Style Steamed Trout

*2 whole Missouri Trout
with heads attached
1 tbsp ginger, finely minced
1 tbsp salted black beans
1 tbsp garlic, minced
4 scallions
2 tbsp soy sauce
2 tbsp Stone Hill Blush
Vidal Wine
4 wooden chopsticks*

- Score both sides of trout in criss-cross cuts approximately ¼ inch deep and ½ inch apart.
- Combine the ginger, black beans and garlic; mix thoroughly.
- Put 1 tsp of the ginger-bean-garlic mixture in the abdominal cavity of each trout.
- Lay the chopsticks in the bottom of a 9"x14" pan. Lay trout on chopsticks in a head to tail position. Pour soy sauce over fish.
- Divide the remaining ginger-bean-garlic mixture over each trout.
- Slice the scallions into thin slivers; criss-cross them over bean mixture.
- Pour the wine in the bottom of the pan. Cover with aluminum foil and place in a 400 degree oven for 12-15 minutes.
- Remove the fish from the pan and arrange on a platter.
- Pour any remaining sauce over the fish and serve.
- Serves 2 as a main course or 8 as an appetizer.

Bass Creole

*2 lbs Missouri Bass Steaks
freshly ground pepper
salt
½ cup green pepper, finely chopped
3 large tomatoes, peeled, seeded,
chopped
6 tbsp butter
2 tbsp syrup from Aunt Nene's
Cracklin'Crisp Bread and
Butter Pickles
⅛ tsp hot pepper sauce
1 tbsp lemon juice*

- Preheat oven to 400 degrees.
- Butter shallow baking dish large enough to hold fish in one layer. Season with salt and pepper to taste. Arrange fish and vegetables in baking dish.
- Melt the butter with the syrup from the pickles, and the hot pepper sauce and lemon juice.
- Drizzle it over the fish.
- Bake 25 minutes, basting with pan juices every 10 minutes.
- Serves 4-6.

Grilled Trout With Two Sauces

4 whole, cleaned rainbow trout
Walnut Butter Sauce (recipe
follows) or Tarragon Cream Sauce
(recipe follows)
Kingsford ® Charcoal Briquets with
Mesquite

- Grill fish on well-oiled grid or in well-oiled wire grill basket, on covered grill, over medium hot briquets 3 to 5 minutes or until fish flakes easily when tested with fork; turn once.
- Serve with Walnut Butter Sauce or Tarragon Cream Sauce.

Walnut Butter Sauce

½ cup Missouri Dandy Walnuts
½ cup butter
3 tbsp Madiera wine

- Saute walnuts in 2 tbsp butter.
- Reduce heat; add remaining butter, stir until melted.
- Stir in wine.
- Serve warm.

Tarragon Cream Sauce

¼ cup olive or vegetable oil
¼ cup Mid-America Farms
Whipping Cream
1 tbsp Progresso Red Wine Vinegar
1 tbsp parsley, finely chopped
1 egg yolk, beaten
½ tsp dried tarragon
¼ tsp pepper
1 small garlic clove, minced.

- Combine all ingredients in bowl; beat with wire whip.
- Serve cool.

In the Ozarks, as far as spear fishing is concerned, there has long been a friendly rivalry between churn giggers and pitchin' giggers.

A churn gig is a 14-foot pinewood pole with three sharp tempered tines attached to it.

A variation, derived from the Osage Indians, uses a true four to five foot spear with only one point, referred to as a pitchin' gig.

They both gig for suckers—redhorse and white sucker mainly—which Ozark streams nurture plentifully, practicing a sport that demands calm, crystal clear water.

Poached Trout With Basil and White Wine Vinaigrette

1 carrot
1 onion
1 whole lemon plus juice from 2 lemons
2 Rainbow Trout, about 12 oz each
⅓ cup extra virgin olive oil
6 fresh basil leaves, minced
⅛ tsp each salt and pepper
1 tbsp capers
⅓ cup tomatoes, skinned, seeded and minced
2 tbsp Mission Creek Dry White Wine
1 clove garlic, minced

To make the marinade:

- To make a court bouillon, fill a fish poacher or other oblong pan with 1 inch of water.
- Add the carrot and onion.
- Squeeze the juice from lemon and add the juice, pulp and rind to the court bouillon. Bring to boil.
- Poach the fish in the boiling bouillon for 10-12 minutes.
- Remove the fish from the pan. Carefully remove the heads, tails, fins, skin and bones so that you have cooked filets.
- Arrange the filets on an oval platter.
- Combine all remaining ingredients; pour over trout.
- Place the trout in the refrigerator for 15 minutes to cool and then serve.
- Serves 2.

Winning medals for excellence has long been a tradition for Missouri wineries. During the last half of the 19th century, native wineries achieved international acclaim. Their wines took top honors at prestigious wine competitions, such as the 1851 Vienna World's Fair, where eight of the 12 gold medals were awarded to Missouri Wines.

Not to be outdone, the French began importing the Norton/Cynthiana grape plants which were responsible for most of the award-winning wines. Unfortuneately for the French, the imported plants were accompanied by Phylloxera, a root louse. This tiny microscopic pest lives in harmony with most native American grape varieties, but utterly destroys the Vinifera grape family, the classic European varieties such as Cabernet Sauvignon and Chardonnay.

By 1880 most French vineyards were devastated by Phylloxera and many European neighbors were threatened. At this time in Missouri, Hermann Jaeger, a winemaker from Neosho, and UMC Professor George Hussman developed a cure for the plague. They found that grafting the sensitive vines onto hardy American root stacks created an immunity to Phylloxera without any noticeable change in wine flavor.

Between 1885 and 1890, Missouri sent an estimated 10 million root stocks to France and literally saved its wine industry. A very grateful French government awarded Jaeger the Cross of the Legion on Honor and the National Order of Knighthood in 1889.

Marking these events' 100th anniversary, a label unveiling and wine tasting was held on November 17, 1989, at the Circle Gallery in Clayton, Missouri. A special commemorative wine, Heritage, was bottled by O'Vallon Winery, a Missouri gold-medal winning winery. Proceeds from the evening were donated to the Hermann Jaeger Memorial Vineyard, a living museum featuring the famous wild grapes and hybrids that saved the wineyards of Europe a century ago.

In March 1990, a group of Missouri's loyal supporters and winemakers departed for a fact-finding tour of France to trace the path of root stock plantings. In Montpillier, a small town in southern France where the root stocks first arrived, there is a statue of a young woman holding an older woman in her arms.

An inscription below thanks the Missouri wine industry for saving the French wineyards. Literally tens of thousands of acres of French-American hybrids are planted throughout France and other wine making of varieties such as Seyval Blanc, Vidal Blanc and Chancellor, the same grapes that are making Missouri wine production famous once again.

Crabmeat Casserole

1 cup heavy cream	• Preheat over to 350 degrees.
1 cup mayonnaise	• Butter shallow baking dish.
1 tbsp parsley, minced	• Combine cream, mayonnaise, parsley, onion, syrup from the pickles, salt, pepper, crabmeat and chopped egg.
1 tbsp onion, minced	
1 tbsp syrup from Aunt Nene's Cracklin'Crisp Bread & Butter Pickles	
salt	• Toss lightly, put into baking dish and sprinkle with buttered bread crumbs.
freshly ground pepper	
3½ cups crabmeat	
6 eggs, boiled and chopped	• Bake for 30 minutes.
1 cup buttered bread crumbs	• Serve 6-8.

An Englishman, Samuel Bowen, was the first to cultivate soybeans in North America. A former seaman, Bowen had been imprisoned in China and observed the many uses of the bean. In 1766 he planted soybeans on his Georgia farm, and then processed them into soy sauce and thin noodles, which he successfully exported to England.

Benjamin Franklin learned about the "magic bean" from the writings of Domingo Navarrete, a priest who wrote about the Chinese bean curt. In 1770, Franklin sent some soybean seeds to a Philadelphia friend, praising the remarkable Chinese "cheese."

The first soybean specialist in the U.S. was botanist William Morse, who with fellow botanist, P. Howard Dorsett, worked from 1929 until 1931 in China and Japan collecting 10,000 soybean varieties for research in the U.S. George Washington Carver was among the first to discover creative uses of the soybean.

Four-H makes a difference in the lives of thousands of youths. Testimony to this comes from the members themselves:

As one says, "I was not interested in anything much until I got involved with 4-H, and then my life seemed to change. I would probably have dropped out of school like my brothers did. Instead of giving up, I discovered that someone besides my parents believed I could do better. I learned that if I wanted to do better, I needed to start believing in myself as well. I went from F's to D's to graduating with a 3.5 average. Plans to attend college this fall are on schedule."

Catawba Bar-B-Q Baste

½ stick Mid-America Farms
Butter, melted
½ cup Meramec Vineyards
Catawba Grape Juice
1 clove garlic, crushed
1 tsp Herb Gathering Thyme
1 tsp Herb Gathering Basil

• Mix all ingredients together.
• Baste while grilling fish, chicken or pork.

Pasta

Rich Meat Sauce for Pasta

4 slices Volpi Pancetta, diced
1 tbsp butter
1 onion, finely chopped
1 carrot, diced
1 stalk celery, diced
¼ lb ground beef, lean
¾ lb Volpi Prosciutto, chopped
¼ cup dry white wine
1¼ cups beef broth
1 tbsp tomato paste
salt and pepper
nutmeg, grated
2 tbsp light cream

- Saute the pancetta in a large saucepan until crisp.
- Add the butter, onion, carrot and celery and cook over low heat stirring frequently.
- Add the meat and cook, stirring, until browned.
- Stir in the prosciutto and the wine.
- Bring to a boil and simmer rapidly until the liquid has almost completely evaporated.
- Stir in the broth and tomato paste and season to taste with salt, pepper and nutmeg.
- Bring to a boil, cover and simmer for 1 hour, stirring occasionally.
- Check the seasoning and stir in the cream.
- Serve with tagliatelli, spaghetti or other pasta.
- Makes about 2½ cups.

When John and Anthony Tumminello opened a small Pizza Parlor Deli in November 1980 for their mother, Lucille, they began making her "dream come true."

Lucille Tumminello, known affectionately as "Mama Lucia," had a life-long dream for her special pizzas. She had made delicious pizzas in her home for over 40 years, preparing several at a time, and placing them in her freezer until her family wanted a snack or dinner.

Three months after her retirement from a 25-year career as a grocery checker in a well-known food chain, Mama Lucia's sons opened the pizza parlor for her. As she prepared her daily pizzas, she placed several in the freezer. Later, she served some of the frozen pizza to her regular customers, and was surprised at their reactions. "I can't believe I'm eating a frozen pizza! This tastes just like the ones you make fresh," was their constant reply.

Soon the customers began ordering several of the frozen pizzas to take home. Mama Lucia's pizzas became Lucia's Pizza and was introduced in small independent grocery stores. Through word-of-mouth and product demonstrations, demand grew so rapidly that bulk orders began arriving from large food chains. In June 1981, only eight months after its inception, Lucia's Pizza Company converted into a strictly 100% wholesale business.

What makes Mama Lucia's pizza different from all the other frozen pizza? Most agree it's her thin, fresh-tasting crust. She uses all natural ingredients and adds no preservatives. Mama Lucia has the only frozen pizza on the market with 100% real provel cheese, a blend of Swiss, Cheddar and provolone.

Lucille Tumminello still watches over the quality of her pizzas. When she comes into the plant, it's not unusual for her to take a pizza off the production line and cook it.

As Mama Lucia says, "Taste is the true test."

Pizza Spaghetti Pie

Meat Layer:
1 lb ground beef
½ cup bread crumbs
½ cup onion, chopped
salt and pepper to taste
⅔ cup Fairmont Milk

Spaghetti Layer:
4 oz spaghetti, cooked
1 egg, beaten
½ cup Parmesan cheese
2 tbsp Mid-America Farms Butter

Topping:
1 (8 oz) can pasta sauce
1 cup Mid-America Mozzarella Cheese, grated

- Combine beef, bread crumbs, onion, salt, pepper and milk.
- Press mixture firmly into bottom of a 9" pie plate.
- Bake at 350 degrees for 35 minutes.
- Spoon off drippings.
- Combine spaghetti with egg, Parmesan cheese and butter.
- Spread over baked meat.
- Top with sauce, mozzarella cheese.
- Bake an additional 10 minutes. Let stand 5 minutes before cutting.
- Serves 4.
- Double ingredients and bake in a 9"x13" pan to serve 8.

The 90s find Missouri facing problems of poverty, substance abuse, teenage pregnancy, parental abuse and neglect, and low youth self-esteem. Unemployment and homicide are abnormally high among black youth.

Missouri 4-H Clubs are answering the challenge to make a difference in the lives of Missouri's young. Four-H Youth Specialists and Youth Education Specialists provide leadership in communities dealing with these problems. Altogether 136,300 boys and girls were enrolled in 4-H education programs totaling 1.4 million hours of study and enrichment during the year ending August 31, 1990.

Missouri 4-H Club members are a mixture of cultures—white, black, hispanic, Asian, American Indian, and others. More than 38% of its members live in suburbs and cities of over 50,000, 48% live in towns of under 50,000, and 13% live on farms.

Nearly 14,000 adult and teen volunteers guide these young members as teachers, mentors, coaches, managers and coordinators, representing a volunteer in-kind contribution of $5,000,000 annually.

Pasta Salad

1 (12 oz) pkg rotelle noodles,
tri-colored
12 oz Alewel's Smoked
Summer Sausage
1 (6 oz) jar marinated
artichokes, cut in half
1 large can whole ripe olives,
sliced
1 green pepper, cut in thin strips
1 red pepper, cut in thin strips
8 oz cherry tomatoes, cut in half
1 bunch green onions, sliced
8 oz fresh mushrooms, sliced
1 head broccoli, cut into small
flowerettes
12 oz Mid-America Farms
Mozzarella, cubed
¼ cup Parmesan cheese, grated
Herb Vinaigrette

- Cook noodles according to package directions, drain.
- Remove casting from summer sausage and cut into thin slices, then into strips.
- Mix all ingredients with Herb Vinaigrette.
- Chill before serving.
- Serves 15 to 20.

Herb Vinaigrette

2 tbsp Dijon-style mustard
½ cup Herbal Design Purple
Basil Vinegar
2 tsp sugar
1 tsp salt
1 tsp black pepper,
freshly ground
fresh parsley, minced
oregano, thyme, chives
or other herbs to taste
1 cup Progresso Olive Oil

- Measure mustard into a bowl.
- Whisk in vinegar, sugar, salt, pepper and herbs.
- Continue to whisk mixture while slowly dribbling in olive oil until mixture thickens.
- Adjust seasoning to taste.

Baked Shells Florentine

½ lb Italian sausage
10 oz frozen spinach, thawed, well-drained
1 cup Breakstones® Smooth and Creamy Cottage Cheese
1 egg, beaten
1 garlic clove, minced
½ tsp dried oregano leaves, crushed
¼ tsp salt
dash of pepper
4 oz large shell macaroni, cooked, drained
8 oz tomato sauce
½ cup 100% Natural Kraft® Low Moisture Part Skim Mozzarella Cheese, shredded
2 tbsp Kraft® 100% Grated Parmesan Cheese

- Preheat oven to 350 degrees.
- Remove sausage from casing; crumble. Brown sausage; drain.
- Add spinach, cottage cheese, egg and seasonings; mix lightly.
- Fill each shell with approximately ¼ cup sausage mixture.
- Place in 10″x6″ baking dish.
- Pour tomato sauce over shells. Sprinkle with remaining ingredients.
- Bake 25 minutes or until thoroughly heated.

Paglia & Fieno

Green and Yellow Fettuccine with egg and prosciutto

¼ lb Volpi Prosciutto, julienned
¼ cup onion, chopped
1 clove garlic, minced
2 tbsp olive oil
½ lb egg fettuccine, cooked and drained
½ lb spinach fettuccine, cooked and drained
½ cup heavy cream
2 eggs, beaten
¾ tbsp salt
¼ tsp pepper
1 medium tomato, diced
Parmesan cheese

- Saute prosciutto, onion and garlic in oil about 5 minutes.
- Add pasta and cream; cook 3 minutes.
- Remove from heat; stir in eggs, salt and pepper, tossing until evenly coated.
- Garnish with tomato and serve with Parmesan cheese.
- Serves 4-6.

Fettuccine with Salsa Verde

8 oz fettuccine, uncooked
1 slice French bread, crumbled
1 clove garlic, peeled
1 tsp sweet basil, dried
2 cups fresh parsley, stems removed
½ cup soybean oil
2 tbsp Herbal Design Mixed Herb Vinegar
1 tomato, peeled, seeded and chopped

- Cook fettucini according to package directions, omitting salt in the water.
- In an electric blender or food processor, combine bread, garlic, basil, parsley, soybean oil and vinegar.
- Process on and off until mixture is well blended and pureed.
- Drain and rinse pasta. Place on a serving platter.
- Spoon salsa over hot pasta.
- Sprinkle with chopped tomato.
- Serve immediately.
- Serves 6.

Manicotti

1½ cups Hudson Chicken, cooked and shredded
1 pkg (10 oz) frozen chopped spinach, cooked and well drained
1 container (16 oz) ricotta cheese
1¼ cups half and half
½ cup Progresso Bread Crumbs
½ tsp basil, dried
½ tsp oregano, dried
1 tsp garlic powder
½ tsp salt
¼ tsp black pepper, ground
1 pkg (8 oz; 14 count) LaBella Manicotti Noodles, prepared
1 jar (15½ oz) Progresso Marinara Sauce
1½ cups (6 oz) mozzarella cheese, shredded

- Preheat oven to 350 degrees.
- In a large bowl, combine chicken, spinach, ricotta cheese, ½ cup half and half, bread crumbs and spices.
- Stuff mixture into manicotti and arrange in a 13"x9"x2" baking dish.
- Combine marinara sauce and remaining ¾ cup half and half, pour over stuffed manicotti; top with cheese.
- Bake for 30 minutes.
- Serves 6.

At 17, Roy Pittrich, Cole County, was left to manage his family's 240-acre farm upon the death of his father. He developed a registered herd of Aberdeen Angus valued in 1941 at $1,275. Roy credited 4-H Club work, his mother's support, his grandfather's counsel, and his close relationship with his county agent with giving him the ability and desire to successfully manage the farm while still a teen-ager.

Fusilli Vinaigrette with Cheese

1 pkg Pasta LaBella Fusilli Grandi
1 cup tomatoes, diced
½ cup frozen green peas, thawed
6 oz mozzarella or provolone, cut in small cubes
1½ tbsp fresh basil, chopped
3 tbsp olive oil
3 tbsp Herbal Design Vinegar from Flavors of the Heartland
salt and pepper to taste
¼ cup Parmesan cheese, freshly grated

- Cook pasta according to package directions. When pasta is "al dente", drain.
- Rinse to stop cooking.
- Place in large mixing bowl. Add tomatoes, peas, cheese and basil.
- Toss mixture well.
- Add oil and vinegar.
- Salt and pepper to taste.
- Toss well, sprinkle with parmesan and serve.

St. Louis began life as a fur-trading enclave on the west bank of the Mississippi, some eighteen miles below the confluence of the Missouri River. It was named for the French King Louis IX, who lived from 1214 to 1270. He was a benevolent ruler, commanding widespread respect from his subjects for wise financial dealings, for initiating direct appeal to the French Crown in legal matters, and for promoting prosperity and peace. He was canonized "Saint Louis" to honor his zeal in pursuing the Seventh Crusade, a commitment which ultimately led to his death.

In the spring of 1811, floods wracked the Mississippi and Ohio valleys, and citizens suspiciously dubbed it the "year of waters." In September, a brilliant comet flashed across the sky, and it was feared that such natural phenomena had ominous overtones.

How ominous became all too clear when, early on a frigid December morning, the earth began to shake violently, and the river tossed and churned ferociously. Trees cracked and fell like splinters into the roaring Mississippi. And the atmosphere was so completely saturated with sulphurous vapors that daylight faded away and darkness hid the sun.

The town of New Madrid in Missouri's bootheel region, known as a strategic gateway to the west, was near the center of the earthquake. One of its residents witnessed that day of terror, and she wrote: "The waters of the river gathered up like a mountain, rising 15 to 20 feet perpendicularly, then receding within its banks with such violence that it took whole groves of cottonwoods which edged its borders. Fissures in the earth vomited forth sand and water, some closing again immediately."

Vast acres of dense, tree-studded land crashed and collapsed inward, submerged under the gush of torrential swells, and new banks were created along the old Mississippi, changing the face of the land dramatically and forever.

Double-Good Macaroni and Cheese

1 lb LaBella Elbow Macaroni
1 lb Central Dairy Cottage Cheese, cream style
1 cup Central Dairy Sour Cream
2 eggs, slightly beaten
1 tsp salt
⅛ tsp pepper
2 tsp onion, grated
1 lb Morningland Dairy Sharp Cheddar Cheese, grated

- Cook macaroni and drain.
- Combine cottage cheese, sour cream, egg, salt, pepper, onion and Cheddar cheese in a large bowl. Mix lightly until blended. Then, fold in macaroni.
- Bake in moderate oven at 350 degrees for 45 minutes, or until bubbly.
- Serves 8.

Missouri's ethnicity shines throughout the state with its many annual fairs and celebrations.

The German "gemutlichkeit," good natured genialty, envelops the reveler in St. Louis' Strassenfest, in Hermann's Maifest, and the ubiquitous Oktoberfests. The French "Feast Days" come alive in St. Charles' Fete des Petites Cotes and at Ste. Genevieve's Jour de Fete.

And Missouri's rich musical heritage is celebrated with Kansas City's Jazz Festival, St. Louis' National Ragtime Festival, and Kahoka's Festival of Bluegrass Music. Branson hosts more than a dozen happy-go-lucky, down-home, foot-stomping, hand-clapping country and gospel music shows. Edgerton, Independence, Osage Beach, Warsaw, Laurie, and Lampe all have their own old-fashioned oprys, jubilees, or music reviews.

Sausage with Vegetables and Fettuccine

1 (12 oz) roll Farmland Sausage
1 garlic clove, minced
1 medium onion, chopped
1 green pepper, chopped
2 cups fresh mushrooms, sliced
1 medium zucchini, sliced,
(about 3 cups)
1 (14 oz) can whole tomatoes,
coarsely chopped
1 tsp basil, dried
1 tsp thyme, dried
½ tsp oregano, dried
¼ tsp black pepper, ground
12 oz Mangia Italiano Fettuccine
¼ cup Parmesan cheese

- In large nonstick skillet, brown crumbled sausage. Remove from skillet and drain.
- Remove all but 1 tbsp of fat from skillet.
- Add garlic, onion, green pepper, mushrooms and zucchini, saute 5 minutes.
- Add tomatoes, with liquid, along with basil, thyme, oregano, pepper and sausage. Stir thoroughly.
- Cover and simmer 10 minutes.
- Cook fettuccine in 4 qts water, 6 to 8 minutes.
- Cook, uncovered, 6-8 minutes, or just until tender, stirring occasionally.
- Drain; rinse with warm water.
- Toss pasta and sausage with vegetable mixture gently.
- Sprinkle with Parmesan cheese.
- Serves 6.

Cheesy Baked Lasagna

½ of a (1 lb) pkg of lasagna, uncooked
1 lb bulk Volpi Abruzzesse Italian Sausage
½ cup onion, chopped
1 clove garlic, minced
1 (15 oz) can Progresso Tomato Sauce, divided
2 (6 oz) cans tomato paste
1½ cups hot water
1 tsp basil leaves
1 tsp oregano leaves
½ tsp marjoram leaves
1 (16 oz) container ricotta cheese
1 (10 oz) pkg frozen spinach, chopped, thawed, and well drained
½ cup Progresso Parmesan Cheese
2 eggs, beaten
½ teaspoon salt
2 cups mozzarella cheese, shredded
2 cups muenster cheese, shredded

- Prepare lasagna according to package directions; drain.
- In medium skillet, combine sausage, onion and garlic. Cook until sausage is no longer pink, stirring often to break sausage apart; drain.
- Reserve ⅔ cup tomato sauce.
- Stir remaining tomato sauce, tomato paste, water, basil, oregano and marjoram into meat mixture.
- Bring to boil. Reduce heat; simmer 5 minutes.
- In medium bowl, combine ricotta, spinach, Parmesan, eggs and salt; mix well.
- In 13"x9" baking pan, spread reserved ⅔ cup tomato sauce.
- Layer one-third *each* lasagna, meat mixture, ricotta mixture, mozzarella and muenster cheeses. Repeat layers.
- Cover. Bake in a 350 degree oven until hot an bubbly, 40-50 minutes.
- Let stand 10 minutes before cutting.
- Refrigerate leftovers.
- Serves 12.

At the turn of the century, John Volpi, thoroughly trained in the salumifici of Milano, Italy, settled in America's heartland.

After researching the most outstanding meats in the U.S., Volpi began creating premium Italian meats in 1902. Combining his experience with unequaled dedication, Volpi was able to recreate the fine Italian delicacies he had known in his native homeland.

This tradition of art and experience to produce a premiere quality product is the driving force behind John Volpi & Company. State-of-the-art technology allows his descendants to continue producing the highest quality prosciutto, pancetta, coppa, pepperoni and the many varieties of salami that have made the company famous.

John Volpi & Company brought the "taste of Italy" home to St. Louis.

Spaghetti alla Carbonara

¾ lb LaBella Spaghetti
½ lb Volpi Pancetta or Prosciutto,
chopped
3 eggs
3 tbsp heavy cream
½ cup Parmesan cheese
salt and pepper
3 tbsp butter

- Cook the spaghetti in boiling water until al dente. Meanwhile, cook the pancetta or prosciutto until crisp. Drain well.
- Beat the eggs with the cream, cheese, a little salt and plenty of pepper.
- Melt the butter in a large saucepan.
- Add the egg mixture and stir until just beginning to thicken.
- Add the drained spaghetti and cooked meat, mix well and serve immediately.
- Serves 4.

Pollo Saltimbocca

6 *whole Hudson Chicken Breasts*
6 *Volpi Prosciutto, thin slices*
(thin ham can be substituted)
1 *slice Caccicavallo Cheese*
2 *eggs*
1 *cup Progresso Bread Crumbs*
½ *tsp black pepper, fine ground*
¼ *cup olive oil, extra virgin*
⅛ *cup Stone Hill Vidal Wine*
1 *lemon, squeezed for juice*
1 *lemon, cut into wedges*
fresh parsley, finely chopped
8 *oz pasta, cooked*

- Skin and bone chicken breasts.
- Remove the small filet from the underside of the chicken breasts.
- Place a half of a chicken breast between 2 pieces of plastic wrap and pound until the meat is about ¼" thick and has been expanded to 4"x5".
- Cut each slice of prosciutto in half and lay a half slice of prosciutto on top of each half chicken breast.
- Divide the slice of caccicavallo cheese into 12 pieces. Each piece of cheese should be approximately ½"x2"x¼".
- Place 1 piece of cheese on top of the prosciutto at one edge of a chicken breast.
- Roll the chicken breast around prosciutto and cheese.
- Beat the eggs.
- Dip the chicken roll into egg, coating all sides and ends, then place immediately in the bread crumbs and roll. Continue rolling in the original direction so breast does not come unrolled.
- Heat the olive oil until it just begins to vaporize, add the chicken breasts with the seam side down. Roll them to right; brown. Again roll to right and brown. Continue until all sides are brown.
- Add wine, cover and cook for 5 minutes.
- Remove to a heated platter.
- Squeeze the lemon juice on top of chicken.
- Garnish with fresh parsley and lemon wedges.
- Serve with pasta.
- Serves 6.

Eggplant and Salami Shells

1½ lbs eggplant, peeled and cut into ½-inch pieces
1 tsp salt
2 (2 oz) jars pimento, drained
⅓ cup chicken broth
¼ cup olive oil
1 clove garlic, minced
2 tbsp fresh basil, minced
1 tbsp fresh lemon juice
½ tsp salt
½ tsp freshly ground pepper
1 small onion, chopped
3 tbsp olive oil
1 (15 oz) container ricotta cheese
¾ cup Genoa salami, chopped
1 cup mozzarella cheese, coarsely grated
3 tbsp Parmesan cheese
1 large egg
⅓ cup fresh basil, minced
¾ lb dried jumbo pasta shells

- Preheat oven to 350 degrees.
- Toss eggplant with salt in a colander.
- Cover with a plate and press; let drain for 30 minutes.
- In a blender, puree pimento with broth, ¼ cup olive oil, garlic, 2 tbsp basil, lemon juice, salt and pepper.
- Store sauce, covered.
- In a large skillet over moderate heat, cook onion in 3 tbsp olive oil until soft.
- Add eggplant and cook until thoroughly heated.
- In a bowl, combine ricotta, salami, mozzarella, Parmesan, egg, ⅓ cup basil and eggplant mixture.
- Cook shells in boiling water until al dente; drain.
- Spread half of sauce in bottom of a large baking dish.
- Stuff shells with eggplant mixture and arrange over sauce.
- Bake, tightly covered, for 30 minutes.
- Serve with remaining sauce.
- Serves 4-6.

On superstitions of the heart, the Ozarker of old believed in some pretty potent powders and potions appealing to paramours.

To capture the heart of some young man, ladies soaked their fingernails in whiskey, then would offer him a glass of the elixer.

To attract a young lady, mountain men placed a mixture of milk, sugar, and flake whiting in her coffee.

Vegetables

Hot Dog! Potatoes Italiano

1 pkg (1 lb) Farmland Lower Fat, Lower Salt Jumbo Beef or Meat Hot Dogs
2 cups onion, coarsely chopped
2 cups green pepper, coarsely chopped
8 oz small mushrooms, sliced
2 cloves garlic, minced
2 (16 oz) cans no-salt-added tomato sauce
1 tsp sugar
2 tsp basil, dried, crushed
1½ teaspoons oregano, dried, crushed
8 baked potatoes, about 6 oz each
2 cups (8 oz) Mid-America Farms Mozzarella Cheese, shredded (optional)

- Slice hot dogs into ¼" pieces; place in a stockpot.
- Add all other ingredients except potatoes and cheese.
- Stirring frequently, cook over moderate heat for 10-15 minutes or until green pepper is crisp-tender.
- Place hot, baked potatoes on serving plates. Make slit in top of each; press to open.
- Spoon filling onto potatoes.
- Garnish with cheese, if desired.
- Serves 8.

Did you know. . .

. . . Soybeans are Missouri's number one cash crop.

. . . In 1989, Missouri soybean farmers produced more than 123 million bushels of soybeans, valued at some $675 million.

. . . In 1989, more than four million Missouri acres were in soybeans.

. . . One-half of all soybeans raised in Missouri are exported.

. . . On the average, every Missourian consumes 35-40 pounds of soybean oil a year.

. . . Approximately 75 percent of all vegetable oil used is soybean oil.

. . . Soybean oil is the major ingredient in:

        85 percent of margarines

        70 percent of solid shortenings

        95 percent of prepared dressings

. . . A 60-pound bushel of soybeans will yield about 49 pounds of soybean meal and 11 pounds of soybean oil.

. . . Using soybeans and soybean products is a good way to lower the cost of serving flavorful nutritious meals and to provide variety in meats.

. . . Soybeans contain many vitamins and minerals including calcium, phosphorus, iron, Vitamin A, thiamin and riboflavin.

Pecan Rice Pilaf

¼ cup soybean oil
¾ cup pecans
1 cup celery, sliced
½ cup onion, chopped
1 tsp salt
½ tsp pepper
½ tsp thyme
1½ cups Della Gourmet Rice, uncooked
2½ cups hot chicken stock

- Heat oil in large saucepan.
- Saute pecans, celery and onions until onion is transparent.
- Add seasoning and rice. Mix well.
- Cook 5 minutes; add chicken stock. Cover pan.
- Simmer until rice is tender and all liquid is absorbed, about 30 minutes.
- Serves 6.

*Soybeans have become
the number one cash crop
in Missouri,
with farmers producing
more than $675 million worth
of soybeans
each year.*

Wayne Marti, president of Ott's Food, recalls what 4-H meant to him:

"I was a member of 4-H for six years. What I remember most is learning about livestock, and a particularly ambitious woodworking project.

"Four-H was definitely a learning experience. I got a lot of leadership training, and enjoyed working with peer groups of similar interest."

Plantation Beans

2 (16 oz) cans pork and beans
1 (16 oz) can kidney beans
1 (16 oz) can butter lima beans
¾ cup bacon, cooked and chopped
1 cup onion, chopped (or equivalent of dried onion)
¾ cup Ott's Plantation Barbecue Sauce
¼ cup sugar
3 tbsp Passport Seasonings Vinegar
1 tsp salt
dash black pepper

- Mix together all ingredients in slow cooker.
- Cover and cook on low for 9-10 hours. The longer this simmers, the more the flavors marry, so it may be cooked for a longer period or reheated successfully.
- However, the quick cooking method (using dried onion) is still delicious and may be heated on top of stove or in a 325 degree oven until bubbly.
- As a side dish, serves 8.
- As a main dish, serves 6.

Marinated Green Beans

1 (16 oz) can whole green beans
4-5 strips Burger's Bacon
½ cup Ott's Famous Dressing

- Place green beans in 9"x5" baking pan and top with bacon slices and dressing.
- Marinate in refrigerator at least 1 hour.
- Bake in 350 degree oven for 30 minutes.
- Serves 4-6.

Renne Nance, director of market analysis for Mid-America Dairymen, relates his personal 4-H experience:

"Growing up in rural Arkansas, 4-H offered an opportunity for young people like me to get together on a regular basis.

"I participated on the county 4-H dairy judging team, and showed junior and senior yearling heifers at the county fair. Even though I never won more than a white ribbon at the county fair, my real rewards came in the form of opportunities and becoming more responsible."

"In college, I assisted in the setting up and conducting of 4-H dairy judging activities. Upon graduation from college, I was employed by the Arkansas Cooperative Extension Service as a 4-H agent. Being able to share in the growth, achievements and disappointments of several hundred youth has helped me to realize the importance of those who guided me in my 4-H years."

Corn Zucchini Bake

3 medium zucchinis
¼ cup onion, chopped
2 tbsp Mid-America Farms Butter
1 (10 oz) pkg frozen whole kernel corn, cooked and drained
1 cup Swiss cheese, shredded
2 eggs, beaten
¼ tsp salt
¼ cup Progresso Bread Crumbs
2 tbsp Parmesan cheese
tomato, chopped
parsley, chopped

- Cut unpeeled zucchini into 1" slices.
- Cook covered in small amount of boiling, salted water, 15-20 minutes.
- Drain and mash with fork.
- Cook onion in 1 tbsp butter until tender.
- Combine zucchini, onion, cooked corn, Swiss cheese, eggs and salt.
- Turn mixture into 1-quart casserole dish.
- Combine crumbs, Parmesan cheese and 1 tbsp melted butter. Sprinkle over corn mixture.
- Bake uncovered at 350 degrees until knife inserted in center comes out clean, about 40 minutes.
- Garnish with chopped tomato and parsley.
- Serves 6.

Aunt Nene's Glazed Acorn Squash with Hazelnuts

2 (1¼ lb) acorn squash, halved lengthwise and seeded
¼ cup hazelnuts
4-5 tsp Aunt Nene's Coriander & Honey Jelly/Glaze
3 tbsp unsalted butter
1 tbsp water, warm

- Arrange squash halves cut side down in a 13"x9" baking dish; cover with wax paper.
- Microwave at HIGH, turning dish after 6 minutes, for 12-16 minutes.
- Remove from microwave and let stand 5 minutes.
- Microwave hazelnuts at HIGH for 1-2 minutes.
- Steam hazelnuts in a towel for 3 minutes, rub off skins; chop fine.
- Microwave butter at HIGH for 45 seconds.
- Turn squash halves cut side up; brush with butter.
- Mix warm water and glaze in small bowl.
- Add hazelnuts to mixture, blend; spoon into each squash cavity.
- Sprinkle with salt to taste. Microwave at HIGH for 2-4 minutes until bubbly.
- Dish can also be prepared in a conventional oven.
- Serves 4.

Harold Bell Wright knew the mountains and the people who called them home. He was a preacher who ventured into the Ozarks, got a ob on a farm, and delivered his first sermon in a little log school.

He based his 1907 novel *The Shepherd of The Hills* on the stories he heard, the people he met during his sojourn in the Missouri high country. In time, it sold more than 18 million copies, becoming one of the world's five most widely read books.

Harold Bell Wright would always say of the rugged mountain ranges, "When God looked upon th' work of his hands and called hit good, he war sure a lookin' at this here Ozark Country."

And so He was.

The American Soybean Association, headquartered in St. Louis, represents more than 32,000 soybean farmers by conducting a wide range of promotion, research and educational activities aimed at increasing soybean profits.

Jefferson City is home to the Missouri Soybean Merchandising Council, which last year challenged consumers to find $100 worth of foods in their supermarkets that contained soybean products. Council Director Kenlon Johannes explained, "Registered shoppers were given 10 minutes to find these (soybean) products and, quite frankly, at the end of the spree, shoppers were amazed at what they had missed."

Royal Stuffed Tomatoes

3 large tomatoes
2½ cups bread crumbs
¼ cup onion, chopped
1 tsp basil leaves, dried, crushed
⅓ cup butter or margarine
1 (10 oz) pkg fresh spinach, chopped, cooked, drained
¼ lb Velveeta® Pasteurized Process Cheese Spread, cubed
1 tbsp Kraft® 100% Grated Parmesan Cheese

- Cut tomatoes in half horizontally. Scoop out centers, leaving ¼″ shell; invert shells to drain.
- Cook crumbs, onions and basil in butter in 10″ skillet until lightly browned. Reserve ¼ tsp crumb mixture, add spinach and half of process cheese spread to remaining crumb mixture; mix lightly.
- Place tomatoes in shallow baking dish; fill with spinach mixture.
- Top with combined reserved crumb mixture and Parmesan cheese.
- Bake at 350 degrees for 20 minutes. Top with remaining process cheese spread; continue baking until process cheese spread begins to melt.
- Serves 6.

Henry Ford, the premiere automobile industrialist, experimented with the soybean, planting 300 varieties on his Michigan farm. From his crops, Ford produced enamel and plastics from soybean oil, and converted soybean meal into horn buttons, instrument knobs, distributor cases, window-trim strips and accelerator pedals. Ford wore a $39,000 suit, shirt, tie and hat made from soybean fibers. On November 2, 1940, Ford startled Americans when he wielded an ax on the trunk lid of his "vegetable" car, produced from a highly resilient soybean-derived plastic. Ford gave up the idea of mass-producing "vegetable" cars in 1943 when a goat ate a license plate made of his soybean fiberboard.

Spinach Balls

2 (10 oz) pkgs frozen chopped spinach, thawed, squeezed dry
2 cups herb stuffing mix, crushed
1 cup Parmesan cheese, firmly packed, freshly grated (5 oz wedge)
½ cup (1 stick) butter, melted
4 small green onions, finely chopped
3 eggs

- Combine all ingredients except the sauce in a large bowl and mix well.
- Shape into 1″ balls.
- Cover and refrigerate or freeze until ready to bake.
- Preheat oven to 350 degrees. Put balls on ungreased baking sheet and bake until golden brown, about 10-15 minutes.
- Serve with mustard sauce.

Mustard Sauce:
½ cup dry mustard
½ cup Passport Seasonings White Vinegar
1 egg yolk
¼ cup sugar

- Combine mustard and vinegar in small bowl. Cover and let stand at room temperature for 4 hours.
- Mix sugar and egg yolk in small saucepan. Add mustard/vinegar mixture and cook over low heat, stirring contantly until slightly thickened.
- Cover and refrigerate.
- Serve sauce at room temperature.

Supreme Green Beans

4 cups fresh cut green beans,
cooked, drained
½ lb process cheese, cubed
½ tsp dill weed
6 slices Farmland Bacon, crispy
cooked, crumbled

- Mix all ingredients except bacon. Spoon into 1 qt casserole; top with bacon.
- Bake 15 minutes at 350 degrees. Stir before serving.
- Serves 6-8.

Variations:
- Substitute ½ cup sliced almonds, toasted, for bacon.
- Substitute 2 (9 oz) pkg frozen cut green beans, cooked and drained, for fresh green beans.
- Substitute 2 tsp chopped fresh dill for dill weed.

Microwave:
- Mix beans, process cheese spread and dill in 1½ quart casserole. Cover.
- Microwave on High 4 to 6 minutes, or until process cheese spread is melted, stirring every 3 minutes.
- Stir in bacon.

Apple Cheese Casserole

1 can apples, sliced for pie
1 stick Mid-America Farms
Butter, softened
1 cup sugar
½ lb Velveeta® Process Cheese
Spread, softened
¾ cup flour

- Spread apples in 1¼ qt casserole dish. Cream butter and sugar, then add Velveeta and cream again.
- Add flour, mix until smooth. Spread batter over apples.
- Bake at 350 degrees for 35-40 minutes.

Creamy Grilled Potatoes

5 medium potatoes, peeled and
thinly sliced
1 medium onion, sliced
6 tbsp butter or margarine
⅓ cup Morningland Dairy
Cheddar Cheese, shredded
2 tbsp parsley, minced
2 tbsp Worcestershire sauce
salt and pepper to taste
⅓ cup chicken broth
2 tbsp bacon bits

- Place sliced potatoes and onion on 22"x18" piece of heavy-duty foil.
- Dot with butter. Sprinkle with cheese, parsley, Worchestershire sauce, salt and pepper.
- Fold up foil around potatoes; add chicken broth.
- Sprinkle with bacon bits. Seal edges tightly.
- Grill packet, on covered grill, over medium-hot Kingsford briquets about 35 minutes or until potatoes are tender.
- Serves 6.

Ozark Grits Casserole

4 cups water
½ tsp salt
1 cup grits
2 eggs
milk
1 stick butter
6 oz Morningland Dairy Garlic
Colby Cheese, grated

- Add grits to boiling water and salt.
- Cook until grits are tender.
- Add butter and all but 2 tbsp garlic cheese.
- Drop eggs into measuring cup and fill with milk to make 1 cup.
- Blend with cooked grits.
- Place mixture in casserole and bake at 350 degrees for 45 minutes.
- Take from oven and sprinkle with remaining grated cheese.
- Return to oven for additional 10 to 15 minutes or until golden brown.
- Serves 10-12.

In Mountain View, Missouri, Jim and Margie Reiners produce Morningland Dairy Cheese from the fresh milk of their 50 cow Holstein herd. What makes Morningland Dairy so special is that its cheeses are made from organic raw milk, produced without the use of herbicides, pesticides, synthetic fertilizers, synthetic proteins, artificial coloring, insecticides, or synthetic livestock feeds.

On their 80-acre farm in the Missouri Ozarks, Jim, Margie and their daughters, Becky, Anna and Melissa, take great pride and responsibility for their beautiful land. As the Reiners state in their brochure, "Because we put a lot into our farm, we care about our product and we like to see it appreciated.

"Selling our milk to a national corporation that dumped our milk in with hundreds of other farmers' and then marketed it along with the cheese of hundreds of other plants, gave us little satisfaction.

"Our satisfaction is seeing our hard work being appreciated by other people who care about what they eat."

Jim personally grinds his animals' feed each week from a mixture of organic corn, natural protein soybean meal and a balanced mixture of minerals. Margie, the head milker, supplements the diet of individual cows with homeopathic remedies if needed.

Since 1981, the Reiners have produced an [all-natural] vegetarian cheese with a flavor unmatched anywhere. They know exactly what goes into their cheese, as the Morningland Dairy has only organically treated hay fields, corn fields and pastures. A special vacuum packing machine ensures the maximum shelf life and product viability.

Morningland Dairy Cheeses are packaged as Monterey Jack, Hot Pepper Jack, Mild Pepper Jack, Caraway Jack, Italian Jack, Chives Colby, Garlic Colby, Colby, Dill Cheddar, Mild Cheddar, No-Salt Mild Cheddar, Medium Sharp Cheddar and Sharp Cheddar. Margie's organic herb beds are the source for the dill, jalapeno peppers, oregano, garlic and chives used in the special blends.

In this fast-paced, sometimes artificial world, it's refreshing to find the natural Morningland Dairy Cheeses at your Missouri grocers.

Au Gratin Rice

2 tbsp butter
2 tbsp flour
½ tsp salt
pepper
nutmeg
1 cup Hiland Milk
1¼ cups Morningland Dairy
Sharp Cheddar Cheese, grated
1 tsp butter
½ cup onion, chopped
3 cups rice, cooked

- Melt butter in saucepan.
- Stir in flour and cook to boiling.
- Add spices and milk. Cook over low heat until sauce thickens, stirring constantly.
- Remove from heat and stir in 1 cup grated cheese.
- Saute onions in butter.
- Add onions and rice to sauce.
- Stir and pour mixture into 1-qt baking dish.
- Top with remaining grated cheese. Bake 30-35 minutes at 350 degrees.

Festival Fried Rice

½ cup Seitz Bacon, chopped
2 tbsp soybean oil
⅓ cup green onions, including tops, sliced
¼ cup red or green pepper, diced
⅓ cup fresh mushrooms, sliced
¼ cup frozen green peas, thawed
1 egg, beaten
2 cups rice, cooked and chilled
1 tbsp soy sauce

- Heat oil in large skillet over medium heat.
- Stir fry bacon, onions, mushrooms, pepper and peas for 1 minute.
- Remove and set aside.
- Pour egg into skillet and scramble for 30 seconds.
- Add rice and soy sauce, stir 3 minutes.
- Serves 4.

Lemon Rice

5 cups chicken stock
1 tsp salt
2 cloves garlic, minced
2 cups long grain rice
2 tbsp lemon zest, finely grated
4 tbsp fresh parsley, chopped
4 tbsp Central Dairy Butter

- Bring the broth, salt and garlic to a boil in a heavy saucepan.
- Stir in the rice, cover, and simmer until the liquid is absorbed, about 20 minutes.
- Remove from the heat. Stir in the lemon zest and let stand covered for 5 minutes.
- Gently stir in the chopped parsley and butter. Season to taste with salt and pepper. Serve immediately.
- Serves 8-10.

Rice Dollar Pancakes

1 cup sifted flour
1 tsp baking powder
½ tsp baking soda
¼ tsp salt
1 tsp sugar
2 eggs
1 cup Fairmont Buttermilk
3 tbsp melted butter, margarine or oil
½ cup cooked Della Gourmet Rice

- Sift together dry ingredients.
- Beat eggs until light.
- Add milk and butter; mix well.
- Stir in dry ingredients and beat just until smooth.
- Add rice.
- Pour or spoon onto hot griddle, using about 1 tbsp. batter for each cake.
- Cook until bubbles form on top and underside is lightly browned. Turn and brown other side. Turn only once.
- Makes about 3 dozen.

Attacked by the Iroquois and other eastern tribes, the Osage Indians trailed along the Ohio River to its confluence with the great Mississippi. They followed the shoreline's serpentine path to its junction with the Missouri River, then journeyed west, settling by the river that now bears their name. They were the "Little Ones" of the great Osage people.

The Osages created a new homeland for themselves in a wilderness that became Vernon County. Agriculture was added to hunting and gathering to sustain their existence. The tribe planted corn, squash, pumpkin, beans and potatoes. They supplemented their diet with grapes, persimmons, walnuts, pecans, acorns and hickory nuts gathered in the wilds. While tribal women pursued the cultivation and harvesting of crops, the Osage men hunted for deer, wild turkey, prairie chicken, skunk, buffalo and bison.

Risotto Milanese
Rice with saffron

2 qts of homemade meat broth
2 tbsp onions, finely chopped
1 clove garlic
5 tbsp sweet butter
3 tbsp diced Volpi Prosciutto
2 cups raw Italian Arborio rice
1 saffron capsule
½ cup Parmesan cheese, freshly grated

- Bring broth to slow simmer.
- Saute onions and garlic in a heavy bottomed pan with 3 tbsp of butter. As soon as the onions become translucent, add the prosciutto and brown for 2 minutes.
- Add the rice and stir until well coated. Saute lightly for a few moments and then add a ladle full of simmering broth. Continue adding ladlefulls of hot broth as rice dries out, stirring frequently to prevent sticking.
- After 20 minutes, add the saffron. When the saffron has been well blended, finish cooking the rice with the hot broth (if you run out of broth add hot water).
- When the rice is done al dente, taste for salt.
- Add a few twists of pepper to taste and turn off the heat.
- Add 2 tbsp of butter and the cheese; mix thoroughly.
- Spoon into hot platter; serve.
- Serves 4.

The first Territorial Governor of Missouri was an absolute scoundrel.

Or perhaps he was a great con artist who wanted to steal an empire or build one of his own.

James Wilkinson fought alongside Benedict Arnold in the Revolutionary War, then got himself involved in a plot to oust George Washington as the Commander of the American Army.

When the plot was uncovered, Wilkinson deserted, but later rejoined the Continental Army as the head of the Quartermaster Corps.

He was removed when shortages were found in his books.

Wilkinson journeyed west, gave his allegiance to the Spanish Government and became one of its most trusted, most important spies, working his way back into the Army and even becoming its highest ranking general.

Burr recommended him to Thomas Jefferson, and the President appointed Wilkinson as the Governor of the State of Missouri.

At the time, however, he and Burr were plotting to steal the Western lands away from the United States and give them all to Spain.

The deal fell through, and Wilkinson was kicked out of Missouri.

Sour Cream Potato Bake

1 (24 oz) pkg Mr. Dell's Frozen Hash Brown Potatoes
3 tbsp butter
¼ cup Central Dairy Milk
1 cup Central Dairy Sour Cream
½ cup Cheddar cheese, shredded

- Thaw and separate potatoes.
- Mix in butter, milk, sour cream and cheese.
- Pack lightly into greased baking dish.
- Bake at 375 degrees for about 45 minutes, until lightly brown.

An employee of Ott's Food, Georgia Kesterson of Carthage, remembers her 10 years in 4-H:

"My fondest memories are of the friendships and the 4-H camps. We all went to 4-H Week in Columbia each year, and once toured the White House when we went to the National 4-H Center."

"I think it was really special over the years to share the fun, different types of activities, and meet other people who aren't all the same. Having grown up in Avilla, Missouri, population 135, 4-H really helped broaden my views."

Twice Baked Potatoes

4 large potatoes
½ cup low fat yogurt
½ cup Ott's Buttermilk Dressing
3 tbsp fresh or frozen chives
salt and pepper to taste
Parmesan cheese

- Scrub potatoes to clean and dry. Rub lightly with vegetable oil.
- Bake in 350 degree oven 1 hour or until soft.
- While hot, slice top off each potato and scoop out potato, leaving a shell.

- Place potato pulp in mixing bowl. Blend in low fat yogurt and dressing. Add more yogurt and dressing if necessary to correct consistency.
- Blend in chives and salt and pepper to taste. Stuff shells with the potato mixture and top with Parmesan cheese. Bake at 350 degrees for 30 minutes.
- Potatoes may be prepared ahead and refrigerated until time to heat.
- Serves 4.

A newfangled contraption called the automobile made its way to Missouri in the early 1900s.

Kansas City had the first two cars.

And they had a head-on collision on a perfectly uncrowded street on a perfectly clear day.

The drivers were playing chicken, and their speeds were only five miles an hour.

Yummy Yams

4 medium yams or sweet
potatoes
1½ cups water
½ stick Mid-America Farms
Butter
¼ cup brown sugar
½ cup Missouri Dandy
Black Walnuts, chopped
miniature marshmallows to top

- Pare and slice yams or sweet potatoes.
- Cook slowly in water until very tender.
- Mash yams, blend in butter, brown sugar and nuts.
- Pour mixture into 2-qt, lightly greased baking dish. Cover with marshmallows.
- Bake at 300 degrees until marshmallows are melted and lightly browned.
- Serves 4-6.

Four-H projects provide a broad learning experience for its members. Its 1989 programs reflected the following enrollment:

10,722 in Foods Nutrition

960 in Lifetime Sports

1,934 in Health Activities

9,089 in Substance Abuse Education

1,748 in Stress Control

266 in Bacteriology

1,211 in Computers

61,066 in incubation and Embryology

976 in Aerospace

732 in Conservation of Natural Resources

4,688 in Space Technology

Desserts

Italian Butter Cookies

1½ cups (3 sticks)
Mid-America Farms
Unsalted Butter
1 cup Pet Evaporated Milk
1 egg, beaten
2 cups all purpose flour
4 cups corn meal
1 cup granulated sugar
1 tsp salt
2 tsp vanilla extract
¼ cup raisins
½ cup slivered almonds

- Melt butter; set aside.
- Combine evaporated milk and beaten egg; set aside.
- In a large bowl, combine flour, corn meal, sugar and salt; mix well.
- Make a well in the center of the flour mixture and pour in the melted butter and vanilla. By hand, work melted butter into flour mixture until completely mixed.
- Stir in evaporated milk and beaten egg ¼ cup at a time.
- Stir in raisins and almonds.
- Chill dough for 30 minutes or until firm.
- Form balls with approximately 2 tsp of dough. Place on ungreased baking sheet and flatten with the bottom of a glass.
- Bake at 375 degrees for 15 minutes or until edges are browned. Remove to cooling racks.
- Let cool completely before storing in airtight container.
- Makes 8 dozen cookies.

A comment about the Mississippi from Mark Twain's *Life on The Mississippi*:

". . . Considering the Missouri its main branch, it is the longest river in the world—four thousand three hundred miles. It seems safe to say that it is also the crookedest river in the world, since in one part of its journey it uses up one thousand, three hundred miles to cover the same ground the crow would fly over in six hundred and seventy-five."

Chocolate Satin Ice Cream Pie

Chocolate Cookie Crumb Crust:
1¼ cups fine chocolate wafer crumbs
¼ cup finely ground Osage Pecan Co. Toasted Pecans or Walnuts
3 tbsp sugar
6 tbsp unsalted butter, melted

Filling:
1 qt Central Dairy Vanilla Ice Cream, softened
1 (8 oz) jar Flavors of the Heartland Chocolate Satin, warmed
1 qt Central Dairy Chocolate Ice Cream, frozen
½ cup whipping cream, whipped

Garnish:
chopped nuts, marachino cherries, drained with stems

For crust:
- Combine crumbs, nuts and sugar in small bowl.
- Pour melted butter over mixture and toss to blend. Press mixture into 9 or 10 inch pie pan. Cover with plastic wrap; chill 30 minutes.
- Spread half of vanilla ice cream over crust; freeze.
- Drizzle half of the chocolate sauce over the top.
- Spread remaining vanilla ice cream over chocolate sauce. Return to freezer to firm.
- Scoop balls of chocolate ice cream and arrange over vanilla layer. Drizzle with remaining warm chocolate sauce.
- Fill pastry bag with whipped cream; pipe rosettes over pie.
- Garnish with nuts and cherries and serve immediately.
- Pie may be prepared ahead and frozen until serving time.
- Serves 10-12.

Linda's Famous Blueberry Sauce & Ice Cream

3 cups Missouri Blueberries
½ cup sugar
¼ cup orange juice
2 tbsp cornstarch
½ gal Hiland Vanilla
Ice Cream

- Mix all ingredients except ice cream together in a heavy quart saucepan over medium heat. Cook until sauce is thick and clear, stirring often. Makes about 2 cups sauce.
- Pour over individual servings of ice cream.

Microwave:
- Place all ingredients in a glass bowl and cook on high 8-10 minutes, stirring every 2 minutes.

It was a July 4 celebration to end all celebrations. With the Independence Day hoopla of 1896 and the coming of the first train, the townfolk of Cassville had a lot to rejoice about. The new train would connect the town, torn by the ravages of Civil War, to commercial links with the world beyond, even though its tracks ran for only five miles and four hundred feet. And it was called the Cassville & Western Railroad.

From Cassville to Exeter, the chugging iron horse brought pride and prosperity to this productive Ozark valley. An encounter with financial difficulties resulted in new ownership, and the name was changed to the Cassville & Exeter Railroad. Punctual, efficient and determined, with a green and tomato red pullman car, it was dubbed the "Fruit Line" when it carried tons of local produce, and people referred to the train as the "Exeter Excursion" during those times when it shuttled Cassville school children on free rides.

Throughout its 60-year life, the C & E remained as the "World's Shortest Standard Gauge Railroad" ever built in the U.S.A.

There was a time when the mountaineers who nailed their homesteads to the Ozark ridges referred to December 25 as "New Christmas."

"Old Christmas" was celebrated on January 6 and had been for as many years as anyone could remember.

Those mountain families were mostly the descendents of settlers who had come from England, a land that did not accept the Gregorian Calendar until the mid 18th century.

Until Pope Gregory XIII came along, everyone paid homage to the Christ Child on January 6.

The Pope changed it to December 25 in 1582.

England did not recognize the change for almost two hundred years.

And it took another two centuries before word filtered its way back into the hollows of the Ozarks.

Strawberry Squares

1 cup sifted all-purpose flour
¼ cup brown sugar
½ cup Missouri Dandy
Black Walnuts, chopped
½ cup butter, melted
2 egg whites
1 cup sugar, granulated
2 cups strawberries, sliced
2 tbsp lemon juice
1 cup Mid-America Farms
Whipping Cream, whipped

- Mix first 4 ingredients; bake in shallow pan at 350 degrees for 20 minutes.
- Stir occasionally.
- Sprinkle ⅔ crumbs in 13"x9"x2" pan.
- Combine egg whites, granulated sugar, berries, and lemon juice. Beat at high speed about 10 minutes.
- Fold in whipped cream. Spoon over crumbs. Top with remaining crumbs.
- Freeze 6 hours. Serves 12.

Hammons Products Company, a Missouri success story, is proud to be represented in the Missouri 4-H cookbook. Executive Vice President Gus S. Rutledge notes:

"The 4-H pledge has continued to inspire me for approximately 50 years. The four big H's (head, heart, hands and health) when dedicated to a club, community and country can and do create a desire for excellence in youth that lasts a lifetime.

"I will always remember these dedicated county agents going above and beyond the call of duty to instill leadership, excellence, wisdom and knowledge to the youth all across America, through the 4-H program."

Buttered Black Walnut Ice Cream

2 cups Missouri Dandy Black Walnuts
3 tbsp butter
2½ cups sugar
4 tbsp flour
½ tsp salt
5 cups Central Dairy Milk, scalded
6 eggs, beaten
4 cups Central Dairy Cream
4½ tsp vanilla

- Saute black walnuts in the 3 tbsp of butter and cool.
- Combine sugar, flour and salt, slowly stir in hot milk.
- Cook 10 minutes over low heat, stirring constantly.
- Stir small amount of cooked mixture into beaten eggs, return to milk mixture and cook one minute.
- Chill in refrigerator, then pour in freezer and add cream and vanilla.
- Churn in freezer for about 15 minutes, then add black walnuts and finish freezing.

The Central Dairy Company has been a family owned and operated company for more than half a century.

All Central Dairy milk is received fresh from dairy farms in Central Missouri. That's where the slogan "Fresh As A Missouri Morning" originated.

Milk is processed in the Jefferson City, Missouri, plant. Central Dairy Company does everything from the time it receives the milk—from making the plastic bottles to delivery to homes, hospitals, restaurants and businesses.

Central Dairy Company manufactures its high-quality milk and ice cream using state-of-the-art equipment. In addition to the complete milk line, which includes Vitamin D, skim and lowfat, Central Dairy Company produces sour cream and cottage cheese.

A favorite of visitors to Central Dairy Company is the old-fashioned Ice Cream Parlor. Banana splits, ice cream sodas, ice cream cones and other treats have made trips to the Parlor memorable for two generations of Missourians. Recognizing its contribution to the community, the Parlor has become a Central Missouri landmark.

Fresh Peach Ice Cream

4 cups Central Dairy Milk
4 eggs
2 cups sugar
2 tbsp cornstarch
½ tsp salt
4 cups Missouri Peaches, crushed
1 (12 oz) can Pet Evaporated Milk
2 cups Central Dairy Cream

- Scald milk.
- Mix together eggs, sugar, cornstarch and salt.
- Add scalded milk to mixture.
- Cook over medium heat, stirring constantly until mixture thickens enough to lightly coat a silver spoon. Cool.
- Add peaches, evaporated milk and cream.
- Pour into ice cream freezer and follow manufacturers directions.

Arlin Schwinke, a member of the Board of Directors for the Missouri Farm Bureau Federation, is proud of his years spent in the 4-H.

Schwinke said, "Being a member of 4-H was a very valuable experience. You learn a lot. You could write a book about all that it does for you. I just think it gives you a head start in life and in dealing with people."

Divine Dessert

3 egg whites	• Beat egg whites until foamy.
¼ tsp cream of tartar	• Add cream of tartar and beat
1 cup sugar	until stiff.
20 soda crackers, crushed	• Add sugar, and beat. Fold in
1 cup Byrd's Pecans, chopped	crushed crackers, nuts and
1 tsp vanilla	vanilla.
½ pt Mid-America Farm	• Bake in well-buttered glass
Whipping Cream, whipped	9"x12" pan 35 minutes at 325
1 (6 oz) jar Centennial Farms	degrees. Cool in pan.
Preserves (pineapple or apricot)	• Fold preserves into whipped
1 cup coconut	cream.
	• Spread over crust and sprinkle on coconut.
	• Chill several hours or overnight.

Mint Dazzles

2 cups Mrs. Alison's Vanilla Wafers, crushed	• Add melted margarine to crushed wafers.
½ cup margarine, melted	• Spread in 9"x13" shallow
1 stick margarine	dish. Chill.
3 eggs	• Mix: 1 stick margarine, eggs,
3 squares baking chocolate, melted and cooled	chocolate and sugar. Beat until creamy. Spread mixture
1½ cups powdered sugar	over wafer crumbs.
1 cup Mid-America Farms Whipping Cream	• Whip whipping cream.
1 cup small marshmallows	• Fold marshmallows into cream. Spread over mixture carefully.
hard peppermint candy, crushed	• Top with crushed candy.
	• Cover pan and freeze.
	• Serves 12.

Fresh Peach Pie

5 cups fresh Missouri Peaches,
peeled and sliced (about 8
medium size)
¼ cup sugar
½ cup brown sugar
2 tbsp tapioca
dash nutmeg
few grains salt
1 tbsp Mid-America Farms
Butter, cut into bits
1 tsp Mid-America Farms Milk
1 tsp sugar
1 pastry for two crust, 9″ pie

- Mix first 6 ingredients.
- Line 9″ pie pan with pastry.
- Pour in peach mixture. Dot with butter.
- Cover top with top crust.
- Seal and flute edges.
- Make decorative slits in top crust.
- Brush lightly with milk.
- Sprinkle with sugar.
- Bake on lowest rack in oven at 400 degrees for 40-50 minutes.

Fresh Peach Delight

½ cup butter
¼ cup confectioners' sugar
1 cup flour
1 heaping tbsp cornstarch
2 tbsp sugar, granulated
½ cup Missouri Gold
Grape Juice
½ cup raspberry jelly
5 cups fresh Missouri Peaches,
peeled and sliced
whipped cream for garnish

- Cream butter and sugar. Add flour and press in bottom of 9″x9″ pan.
- Bake at 350-400 degrees for 10-15 minutes or until golden brown. Watch closely.
- Next mix cornstarch, sugar, grape juice and raspberry jelly; cook until thick.
- Cool. Arrange sliced peaches on crust (sweeten a little if peaches are very tart).
- Pour cooled mixture over peaches. Cover with plastic wrap or foil and refrigerate.
- Cut in squares and top each serving with whipped cream.
- Serves 9.

The footsteps of thousands
of Missouri's urban and rural youth
are carefully guided
by the programs
of Missouri 4-H.

With majestic trees growing almost 90 feet tall, Missouri is the largest producer of black walnuts in the world.

In October and November, almost half of the world's supply of these tangy-flavored nuts are collected by hand, with Missouri's annual production being roughly 40 million pounds.

Additional to its value as a nutmeat, the wood is desired for furniture. The shell, when ground, produces a soft, gritty abrasive substance that is a key cleaning agent for precision instruments and jet engines, as well as a polish for chrome.

It was, in fact, ground shell from Hammons Products Company that was used to clean the Statue of Liberty.

Missouri Black Walnut and Bourbon Pie

3 eggs
1¼ cups sugar, granulated, divided
4 tbsp cornstarch
5 tbsp bourbon
½ cup butter, melted
1¼ cups Missouri Dandy Black Walnuts, chopped
1 (6 oz) pkg semisweet chocolate morsels
1 (9") unbaked pie shell

- Beat eggs with ¾ cup sugar.
- Mix remaining ½ cup sugar with cornstarch; add to egg mixture.
- Fold in bourbon, butter, walnuts and chocolate morsels.
- Pour filling into unbaked 9" pie shell.
- Bake in a preheated 375 degree oven for 15 minutes.
- Reduce oven temperature to 325 degrees; bake 15 minutes, or until filling is set and crust is golden.
- Yields 1 pie; 6-8 servings.

Hammons Products Company harvests the native eastern black walnuts of Missouri into the "Missouri Dandy" products famous for their taste and quality.

The story of Hammons Products Company is the story of one man's dream. Returning to civilian life after serving in World War II, Ralph Hammons purchased 3 million pounds of nuts and shipped them to a plant in Virginia for processing. The success of this venture, combined with the abundance of black walnuts and the high cost of freight led Ralph to build a processing plant of his own in Stockton, Missouri. The year was 1946, and Hammons Products Company was born.

Still family owned and managed, Hammons Products Company annually processes most of the nation's eastern black walnuts. In addition to the Stockton nutmeat plant, Hammon's has:

– The shell plant which processes the hard outside shell of the nut, producing valuable shell products including paints, explosives, cosmetic cleaners, metal cleaners and polishers, and sealants in oil well drilling.

– The feed plant which utilizes the nutmeats that do not meet Hammon's high quality standards. Mixed with shelled corn, an animal feed of exceptionally high nutritional value is produced.

– The "Missouri Dandy Pantry" which is the mail order and retail sales division, offering a variety of nutmeats and specialty gift items in addition to black walnuts.

– The Land Management Division which conducts research and encourages development of eastern black walnut crops.

Hammon's supplies homemakers and professional bakers alike with natural, unroasted nutmeats to create delicious cakes, cookies, rolls and other baked goods. From fudge to brittle, black walnuts add a distinctive flavor to candies. And who can resist black walnut ice cream, a favorite of connoisseurs everywhere.

Black walnuts are rich in nutrition and high in polyunsaturated fats, protein and carbohydrates. They have no cholesterol, and contain vitamins A, B and C, as well as iron, calcium and riboflavin. Eastern black walnuts are a particular favorite because of their full, robust flavor, when compared to western or California walnuts.

Black Walnut Fudge Pie

2 cups Mid-America Farms
Butter
4 cups sugar
8 oz unsweetened chocolate,
melted
8 eggs
¼ tsp salt
1 cup flour
4 tsp vanilla
2 cups Missouri Dandy Black
Walnuts, coarsely chopped

Filling:
- Whip butter and sugar until light and fluffy.
- Blend in cooled chocolate and eggs.
- Fold in salt and flour.
- Add vanilla and walnuts.
- Pour into unbaked pie shells.
- Bake at 350 degrees 50-60 minutes.

2 cups flour
1 tsp salt
⅔ cup shortening
1 cup Missouri Dandy Black
Walnuts, finely chopped
5-7 tbsp cold water

Pastry:
- Sift flour and salt.
- Cut shortening into flour until mixture is the consistency of coarse meal.
- Add black walnuts.
- Add water, mixing until dough forms a ball.
- Roll on lightly floured pastry cloth or board.
- Yields 2 (9″) crusts.

Fudge Sundae Pie

1 cup Pet Evaporated Milk
1 cup chocolate bits
1 cup miniature marshmallows
¼ tsp salt
1 qt Central Dairy Vanilla
Ice Cream
Mrs. Alison's Vanilla Wafers
¼ cup pecans

- Combine first 4 ingredients and cook over medium heat until ingredients are melted and mixture thickens. Cool.
- Line bottom and sides of 9″ pie pan with vanilla wafers.
- Spoon ½ of ice cream over wafers. Cover with ½ of chocolate mixture. Repeat layer.
- Freeze until firm, 3-5 hours.

Missouri 4-H members helped South Carolinians, devastated by Hurricane Hugo, have a happier holiday season in December 1989.

After receiving a call for aid at the state 4-H office in Columbia, two veteran 4-H volunteers, Don and LaVerne Cwiklowski of St. Charles County, swung into action. Don and LaVerne organized efforts statewide, asking all Missouri 4-H clubs to collect Christmas gifts, household items, clothing and cash in the "4-H Kids Helping Kids" campaign.

The J.H. Ware Trucking Co. of Fulton transported more than $5,000 in cash and a semi-trailer load of gifts and goodies to the South Carolina coast. Toys, books and school supplies were included in the 10,000 gifts that 200 4-H clubs had collected for their Carolina counterparts.

Jo Turner, state 4-H youth specialist, summed it up this way: "The generosity and enthusiasm of everyone involved was heartwarming, but not surprising."

"4-H people are always ready to help others. This project was a wonderful example of how 4-H clubs across Missouri care about others and work to give service to their clubs, community, country and world."

Harvest Grape Pie

4 cups Missouri Grapes
1 cup sugar
3 tbsp flour
1 tsp lemon juice
dash of salt
3 tbsp Meramec Grape Juice
Pastry for 2 crust pie
1 tsp milk
1 tsp sugar

- Slip skins from grapes and bring pulp to a boil.
- Put pulp through a strainer.
- Mix strained pulp with grape skins; add sugar, flour, lemon juice, salt and grape juice.
- Pour mixture into a pastry lined pie pan.
- Add top crust; trim, flute and decorate as desired. (Pastry grape leaves are attractive.)
- Brush crust with milk and sprinkle with sugar.
- Bake at 400 degrees for 40 mins.
- Serves 6-8.

In Kansas City expect the unexpected.

It rises above the heartland of America all right.

But its fountains have a distinct Roman flair.

So much of its grand architecture was definitely influenced by Spain.

And its boulevards are a faithful reflection of those that run through Paris.

Coconut Carmel Pie

¼ cup Daricraft Butter
7 oz coconut
½ cup Midwestern Pecan Co. Pecans
8 oz cream cheese
1 (12 oz) can Pet Evaporated Milk
16 oz whipped topping
2 (9") Pet-Ritz Regular Pie Crust Shells, baked
12 oz caramel topping

• Melt butter; add coconut and pecans.
• Cook until brown. Set aside.
• Combine cream cheese and evaporated milk. Beat until smooth. Fold in whipped topping.
• Layer ½ cheese mixture, ½ caramel topping and ½ coconut mixture.
• Repeat layers, cover and freeze until firm.
• Thaw 5 minutes before serving.
• Makes 2 pies.

Razzle Dazzle Strawberry Pie

1 (7 oz) jar Kraft Marshmallow Creme
1 cup strawberry ice cream, softened
1 (8 oz) container strawberry yogurt
2 cups frozen whipped topping, thawed
1 (9") pie crust, baked

• Mix marshmallow creme and ice cream at medium speed on electric mixer until well blended.
• Stir in yogurt; fold in whipped topping.
• Pour into shell; freeze at least 1 hour.
• Refrigerate 5 minutes before serving.
• Serves 6-8.

It was on the banks of the White River in 1857 when pearl fishing became a respected Missouri profession. A mussel being used as bait for a trotline was opened up, and the fisherman found a pearl glistening inside. He promptly journeyed to St. Louis and showed the gem to a jeweler who bought it for $1,500. The great pearl rush was on.

Many families trekked through the White River's underbrush and encamped on its muddy banks to dig for mussels, prying them open, praying for pearls. So highly regarded for their quality were these White River pearls that they were sold as far away as London and Paris.

Most pearl fishing died out around 1910. An enterprising person suddenly realized that the mother of pearl lining in the mussel shells could be used to create buttons. So the interest switched from fishing to fabrication, and button factories grew up in several Ozark communities.

Double-Apple Tart

Tart Pastry:
1 cup flour
¼ tsp salt
6 tbsp cold butter
1 egg yolk
2 tbsp water

Filling:
3 cups apples, pared, cored, sliced paper-thin
sugar
1½ cups Aunt Nene's Autumn Harvest Marmalade

- Spread marmalade in partially baked tart shell.
- Cover with apples; sprinkle with sugar.
- Bake at 375 degrees until apples are tender.

- Mix flour and salt.
- Cut in butter until mixture resembles coarse meal.
- Whisk egg yolk and 2 tbsp water in another bowl, add to flour mixture. Blend until pastry holds together in a ball.
- Wrap in foil or plastic and refrigerate it for at *least* 20 minutes and roll out.The dough should be thick enough to hold filling, but not too thick around bottom edge or the finished tart will seem coarse.
- Partially bake in 425 degree oven for 6 minutes.
- If time allows, cover the lined pan snugly with foil and refrigerate before filling and baking.

Missouri has many ethnic enclaves in the large cities and throughout the state, in addition to its Indian, French, Spanish, and Anglo inheritance. Its worldwide heritage is reflected in the names of its towns: Alexandria, Amazonia, Amsterdam, Arcadia, Athens, Belgrade, Belgique, Cairo, Caledonia, Canaan, Carthage, Cuba, Edinburg, Elsinore, Glasgow, Herculaneum, Iberia, Lebanon, Palmyra, Paris, Rome, Sparta, Troy, Verona, Vichy, Versailles, and that domain of the Hapsburgs—Vienna.

Streusel Pecan Pie Squares

Crust:
3 cups flour
¾ cup brown sugar, firmly packed
1½ cups of margarine or butter

Filling:
¾ cup brown sugar, firmly packed
1½ cups corn syrup or maple flavored syrup
1 cup Hiland Milk
⅓ cup margarine or butter, melted
1 tsp vanilla
4 eggs
1½ cup Midwestern Pecan Co., Pecans, chopped

- Heat oven to 400 degrees.
- In large bowl, combine all crust ingredients at low speed until crumbly.
- Reserve 2 cups crumb mixture for filling and topping. Press remaining crumb mixture in bottom and ¾" up sides of ungreased 10"x15" jelly roll pan.
- Bake at 400 degrees for 10 minutes.
- In large bowl, combine ¼ cup reserved crumb mixture and all filling ingredients except pecans, mix well.
- Stir in pecans. Pour over prebaked crust, bake additional 10 minutes.
- Reduce oven temperature to 350 degrees.
- Sprinkle remaining 1¾ cups reserved crumb mixture over filling.
- Bake at 350 degrees for 20-25 minutes.
- Yields 15 servings.

Three out of every four acres
in Missouri
more than 30 million acres,
are devoted
to some kind of farming.

Gingerbread

1½ cups all-purpose flour
½ cup sugar
1 tsp baking soda
1 tsp cinnamon
½ tsp ginger
¼ tsp salt
½ cup light molasses
¼ cup Daricraft Butter
¼ cup brown sugar, firmly
packed
1 (5 oz) can Pet Evaporated Milk
1 egg, well beaten

- Preheat oven to 325 degrees
- In a large bowl, stir together flour, sugar, baking soda, cinnamon, ginger and salt.
- In a small saucepan, melt molasses, butter and brown sugar.
- Add evaporated milk to warm mixture, then beat in egg.
- Pour molasses mixture over dry ingredients. Beat with electric mixer on LOW until moistened. Beat on HIGH 2 additional minutes.
- Pour batter into a greased 9″ square baking pan.
- Bake 40-45 minutes or until toothpick inserted near center comes out clean.
- Serve warm; top with Old Fashioned Lemon Sauce.
- Serves 9.

Old Fashioned Lemon Sauce

½ cup butter
1 cup sugar
¼ cup water
1 egg, well beaten
3 tbsp lemon juice
Grated rind of 1 lemon

- Combine all ingredients.
- Cook over medium heat, stirring constantly until boiling.
- Serve warm.
- May be refrigerated and reheated.
- Also a delicious topping for cooked rice, bread pudding, pound cake, etc.
- Yields 1⅓ cups.

The legends of Mark Twain, the landmark Samuel Langhorne Clemens, still cling to the shoreline of the Mississippi River at his hometown of Hannibal.

As a writer, Twain mined his memory, using many of Hannibal's locations for his tales about Tom Sawyer and Huck Finn. On brick-paved Hill Street, which leads to the river, stand both Clemens' boyhood home and the Becky Thatcher House, where his childhood sweetheart Laura Hawkins lived.

Next door, the stone Memorial Museum contains many of Twain's personal items and memorabilia, including the battered cherry desk where he wrote *The Adventures of Tom Sawyer* and *The Adventures of Huckleberry Finn*.

Across the street is the tiny Clemens Law Office where Twain's father once presided as the town's Justice of the Peace. He was, as Twain remembered, "a stern, unbending man of splendid common sense." The room, with its worn wooden floors and weathered furniture, was used in detailing Muff Potter's trial in *Tom Sawyer*.

Steamboats no longer churn their way down the Mississippi. But the Mark Twain Riverboat cruises the Big Muddy.

And less than five miles away is the Mark Twain cave, a favorite childhood haunt, with dark, winding passageways that inspired the cavern where Tom and Becky lost their way. Now tour guides make sure no one else gets lost as they immerse themselves in Twain's American folklore.

Ozark Pudding

2 eggs
1½ cups sugar
4 tbsp flour
2 tsp baking powder
⅛ tsp salt
1 cup Missouri Dandy Black Walnuts
3 Missouri Apples, peeled; diced
1½ tsp vanilla

- Beat eggs and sugar until smooth. (Do not over beat.)
- Add flour, baking powder, salt, apples and vanilla.
- Bake in 8"x10" shallow pan at 350 degrees for 35 minutes.
- Serve with whipped cream or ice cream.

In the twilight of his years, Mark Twain returned to Hannibal. Viewing the mighty Mississippi as it wound past his hometown, he contemplated the region's significance to his life and work.

He remarked, "I recognized then that I was seeing now the most enchanting river view the planet could furnish. I never knew it when I was a boy. It took an educated eye that had traveled over the globe to know and appreciate it."

Fall Harvest Cake

1½ cups sugar
½ cup brown sugar, firmly packed
2 tsp ground cinnamon
2 tsp baking soda
½ tsp salt
¼ tsp nutmeg
¼ tsp ginger (optional)
1 cup soybean oil
½ tsp vanilla
4 eggs
2 cups flour, sifted
1 (16 oz) can pumpkin
1 large apple, peeled and chopped
1½ cups Missouri Dandy Black Walnuts, chopped

Icing:
3½ cups (1 lb) powdered sugar, sifted
½ cup butter, softened
1 (8 oz) pkg cream cheese, softened
2 tsp vanilla

- Preheat oven to 350 degrees.
- Generously grease and flour a bundt pan.
- In a large bowl, thoroughly mix sugars, cinnamon, soda, salt, nutmeg, ginger, oil, vanilla and eggs.
- Add flour ½ cup at a time, beating after each addition.
- Mix in pumpkin.
- Stir in apple and nuts by hand. Pour into prepared bundt pan.
- Bake 70 minutes.
- Cool 20 to 25 minutes.
- Remove from pan.
- Make icing by beating all ingredients until smooth.
- Spread icing on cake.
- Store in refrigerator.
- Serves 12.

Honey Fudge Cake

½ cup butter
¼ cup sugar
¾ cup honey
⅛ tsp salt
½ cup cocoa
1⅓ cup cold water, divided
2½ cups sifted cake flour
1 tsp baking soda
2 tbsp boiling water
3 egg whites
¾ cup sugar

Caramel Pecan Topping
1 jar Flavors of the Heartland
Chocolate Satin Sauce, warmed

- Cream together butter, sugar, honey and salt until light and fluffy.
- Combine cocoa and ⅓ cup water. Add to creamed mixture, blending well. Add cake flour alternately with remaining 1 cup water, beating well after each addition.
- Combine baking soda and 2 tbsp water. Stir into batter.
- Beat egg whites until frothy.
- Gradually beat in ¾ cup sugar. Fold into batter.
- Pour batter into greased and floured 13"x9"x2" baking pan.
- Bake in 350 degree oven for 50 minutes or until cake tests done. Cool in pan on rack.
- Spread cake with caramel pecan topping, and glaze with chocolate sauce.

Caramel Pecan Topping

⅔ cup brown sugar, firmly packed
1½ tsp flour
2 egg yolks
⅔ cup Hiland Milk
1 tbsp butter or margarine
½ cup pecans, chopped

- Combine brown sugar, flour, egg yolks, milk and butter or margarine in heavy 2 quart saucepan.
- Cook over medium heat, stirring occasionally, until thick (about 15 minutes).
- Stir in pecans. Cool.

4-H continues to build character in youths with the help of people like Beth and Roger Wiseman who, for 16 years have inspired more than 400 children to learn and grow.

Their desire to help North St. Louis youth began as a mission of the Inner City Christian Church where Roger worked. They saw teens caught up in a world of drugs, teenage pregnancy, illiteracy and gangs. The Wiseman's were determined to do something about it. Because Beth had been in 4-H for 10 years in Oregon, she knew the value of traditional programs as well as special interest group activities.

At the Wiseman's Northside Center, the family holds 4-H meetings and runs an after school program at the church. Her 4-H'ers have presented demonstrations at 4-H Achievement Day, the State Fair, the Mayor's office, and many have attended camp. The Wiseman programs have received numerous recognitions and awards for youth work and achievement, including the President's Golden Seal Award and the Operation Brightside Award.

On any one day, a cooking lesson may be held in the kitchen, a music lesson in the chapel area, plus arts or crafts in some other room. Volunteers, often former Wiseman 4-H'ers, provide much-needed help to the groups.

As Beth says, "with Jesus, my husband and my children by my side, we will always have a 4-H program. As long as there are kids, our door is always open for 4-H's true meaning—heart, hand, head and health."

Buttermilk Pie

1 stick butter at room temperature
2 cups sugar
3 eggs
2 rounded tbsp flour
1 cup Hiland Buttermilk
dash of nutmeg
1 tsp vanilla or lemon flavoring
1 (9") Pet-Ritz Regular Pie Crust Shell, unbaked

- Cream butter and sugar.
- Add the eggs and flour, mixing well.
- Stir in buttermilk, nutmeg and vanilla.
- Pour into the pie shell and bake at 325 degrees for 1¼ hour.
- This pie freezes well.

Those who called the Ozarks home held fast to the following traditions for generations:

It is good luck for a girl to receive a button as a gift.

It is bad luck to give away yeast.

If one man gives another a knife, it is sure to sever their friendship.

If you find a hairpin in your pathway, you will soon meet a new friend.

Your luck turns bad if you lend someone salt.

You can expect good fortune if you run across a rock with a hole in it, especially if the stone is found in running water.

Wine Cake

1 (1 lb 2½ oz) pkg yellow or white cake mix
1 (3 oz) pkg raspberry or strawberry-flavored gelatin
¾ cup Stone Hill Blush Wine
½ cup Hollywood Safflower Oil
4 eggs, unbeaten

- Combine all ingredients in bowl and beat for about 3 minutes with electric beater.
- Pour into lightly greased and floured 10-inch tube pan or bundt pan.
- Bake in 350 degree oven for 55 to 60 minutes.
- Remove from oven, let stand 5 minutes.
- Turn out on cake rack.
- When cool, spread with thin wine glaze.

Blush Wine Glaze

⅓ cup Stone Hill Blush Wine
2 tbsp Daricraft Butter
2 cups powdered sugar, sifted

- Heat together wine and butter.
- Remove from heat and gradually stir in powdered sugar.
- When cooled and slightly thickened, spread over top cake.

One of America's most respected agricultural scientists was born near Diamond Grove in 1864. His contribution to science was eclipsed only by his contribution to the dignity of his people.

George Washington Carver promoted crop rotation in response to a cotton-weary, nutrient-exhausted land. This, coupled with the arrival of the boll weevil, had virtually devastated cotton crops everywhere.

A religious and self-effacing man, Dr. Carver, in his quest for knowledge, recalled that he once questioned why God had created the universe.

That's too big for you to get a handle on, he said God told him.

So he asked God, "Why did you create man?"

That's too big for you to handle as well, he said God told him. You should narrow the scope of your query somewhat.

So Dr. Carver asked God, "Can you tell me about the peanut."

He said, "God smiled down and told me, now that's just about the right size for you to get a hold of."

In time, Dr. Carver developed 300 extractions from the peanut, including peanut butter.

Black Forest Dessert

1 (8 oz) can crushed pineapple
1 (21 oz) can cherry pie filling
1 devil's food cake mix
1 cup Osage Pecans, chopped
1 stick soy oil margarine, melted

- Drain pineapple and reserve liquid.
- Spread drained pineapple in lightly greased 9"x13" pan.
- Spread pie filling over top of pineapple.
- Sprinkle dry cake mix over filling.
- Sprinkle nuts over top.
- Combine pineapple juice and melted margarine.
- Drizzle over cake.
- Bake in 350 degree oven for 35-40 minutes.

Jolene Allgaier, director of promotion and education, Missouri Soybean Merchandising Council, fondly remembers her 4-H days.

"I really value the time and experiences I had in 4-H. I feel that 4-H helped me grow as a person and mature in all areas. Project work, judging and activities have led me to be more of a perfectionist. Do the job well!"

"People involved in 4-H learn that if you're going to do something, do it to the best of your ability."

Missouri 4-H looks to the future with constant expansion and improving of programs to challenge, educate and prepare its young members. A shift in emphasis is reflected in programs which stress human relations, scientific discoveries, leadership and citizenship development. Concentration of 4-H programs is placed on developing competent and civic-minded young men and women.

As stated in the Missouri 4-H mission statement, "Four-H . . . creating environments in which young people are valued, contributing members of their communities."

Gooey Almond Cake

¾ cup soybean oil margarine, melted (1½ sticks)
1½ cups sugar
2 eggs
pinch of salt
2 tsp almond extract
½ tsp vanilla extract
1½ cups flour
2 tsp sugar
2 tbsp slivered almonds

- Preheat oven to 350 degrees.
- Line an 8 or 9-inch iron skillet with aluminum foil.

- Combine the melted margarine and sugar in a large mixing bowl.
- Beat in the eggs, one at a time. Beat well.
- Add pinch of salt, almond extract and vanilla.
- Stir in flour until ingredients are well blended.
- Pour batter into the foil-lined skillet.
- Sprinkle the remaining sugar and almonds over top of batter.
- Bake at 35-40 minutes until cake is golden brown and tests done.

After nine years with Swift & Co., Edwin H. "Pop" Schnuck invested his family's savings to oipen a wholesale meat business in 1937.

By 1939, the business was thriving, and Pop's two sons, Edward and Donald, were working in the business. A daughter, Annette, also helped out on weekends.

That same year, Anna Donovan "Mom" Schnuck propelled the family into the retail food business by opening a corner confectionery in north St. Louis. Pop's meat business, having outgrown the family home, moved into the back room, which was just large enough to hold a cooler, meat racks and a scale.

Mom Schnuck prepared potato salad and coleslaw with care and quality ingredients to sell in her 1,000 square foot store, which she decorated with fresh flowers. Open seven days a week from 8 a.m. to 9 p.m., the family firm sold staples, fresh meats and ice cream, and in 1940 became a self-service grocery store.

As the Schnucks helped their customers make the transition from a service intensive to a self-service store, they also began delivering groceries. This allowed them to compete with larger markets with more parking space. Because of the convenience, the delivery service encouraged customers to shop for more than they could carry home in their arms, thus enabling Schnucks to get each family's main grocery order.

Quality food products, convenience and attention to personal service became the foundation on which Schnucks continues to build today. From its humble beginnings, Schnuck Markets, Inc. has grown to a current total of 59 stores, and is the undisputed leader in the St. Louis market. The company also operates stores in Cape Girardeau and Columbia, Missouri, in southern and central Illinois, in Evansville, Indiana, and will open its first store in Kansas City in late 1990.

A third generation of the Schnuck family and their associates now manage the company which won the 1989 *Supermarket Business* Magazine's Award for Excellence in retailing.

The Schnucks Bakery plant produces breads, cakes, pies, donuts, rolls and other baked goods which carry the Nancy Anne label. Named after

Don Schnuck's youngest child and only daughter, Nancy Anne products are known for their freshness and flavor, and are proudly represented in the Missouri Department of Agriculture's AgriMissouri program.

Zuccotto

2 Nancy Anne loaf-shaped pound cakes
1 cup butter, softened
1 cup granulated sugar
¼ cup amaretto liqueur
1 tsp Schnucks Vanilla Extract
½ tsp almond extract
6 oz blanched almonds, ground in a blender
6 oz semi-sweet chocolate, melted
2 cups whipping cream

- Cut cakes vertically into pieces about ¼ inch thick. Cut each piece of cake diagonally into 2 triangles.
- Line a 2½-qt bowl with plastic wrap. In an attractive manner, line bottom and sides of bowl with the cake triangles that come from the top of cake having dark brown coloring. (Use brown to form a pattern.) Set bowl aside.
- In a large mixing bowl, with electric mixer, beat butter until fluffy. Slowly beat in sugar. Beat mixture 1 minute.
- Add amaretto, vanilla extract and almond extract. Beat well.
- Stir in almonds, then add, chocolate and stir until blended. Set mixture aside.
- In a medium bowl, with electric mixer, whip cream until stiff. Fold whipped cream into chocolate mixture.
- Put a layer of chocolate mixture in cake-lined bowl. Break remaining cake triangles into large pieces. Add a layer of cake pieces to bowl.
- Continue layering chocolate mixture and cake until bowl is filled, making the last layer a complete covering of cake. If necessary, trim cake that extends over bowl's edge. Wrap top of bowl in plastic wrap.
- Place a weight, which fits just inside bowl, on top of mixture, to compact it. Refrigerate cake, weighted, overnight. Unmold cake onto a pretty serving plate.
- Serves 10.

A mountain man wouldn't dare drive down a road if he saw a whirlwind in it.

But he always expected good luck if he encountered a red-haired girl on a white horse.

It was considered bad luck to put the left foot out of bed in the morning.

A woman mixing a cake always stirred in one direction. To change directions would surely spoil the cake.

And everyone swore that it was impossible for a bad woman to make good applesauce.

Italian Cream Cake

5 eggs (separate yolks and whites)
1 stick Daricraft Butter
½ cup Hollywood Safflower Oil
2 cups sugar
2 cups flour
1 tsp soda
1 cup Osage Pecans or Walnuts
1 cup Mid-America Farms Buttermilk
1 small can coconut
1 tsp vanilla

- Beat the egg whites in a small bowl, set this aside.
- In a large bowl, cream butter, oil and sugar until smooth.
- Add egg yolks. Combine flour, soda and nuts. Add to creamed mixture alternately with buttermilk. Stir in coconut and vanilla. Fold in beaten egg whites.
- Pour into 3 greased and floured cakepans or 2 9" square pans.
- Bake in 350 degree oven 25-30 minutes or until done.

Icing:

1 (8 oz) pkg Philadelphia Cream Cheese
½ stick Daricraft Butter
1 tsp vanilla
1 box powdered sugar
½ cup Osage Pecans or Walnuts, chopped

- Beat cream cheese and butter until smooth.
- Add sugar, vanilla and nuts and beat well.
- Spread on the cooled cake.

Encouraged by the reception to his music in Sedalia, Scott Joplin and his Queen City Negro Band moved on to a bigger musical capital in St. Louis. The band consisted of Joplin's magical piano sound and that of his clarinetist, coronetist, E-flat tubist, and drummer.

It was the eve of the twentieth century, and the stirrings of a new musical genre was seducing St. Louis. The Music was ragtime. The band and Joplin were hot.

He wrote a tune in 1902 called "The Entertainer," and it became the theme song to a motion picture seventy-two years later. The film was "The Sting."

Steinbaugh's Layered Blueberry Cheesecake

1 cup flour
½ cup butter, softened
½ cup Midwestern Pecan Co. Nuts, finely chopped
8 oz cream cheese, softened
1 cup powdered sugar
8 oz whipped topping
3 cups Missouri Blueberries
¼ tsp salt
2 tbsp lemon juice
1 cup sugar
¼ cup water
3 tbsp cornstarch

- Mix flour, butter and nuts; press into 9″ x 13″ baking dish.
- Bake at 350 degrees for 15 minutes.
- Combine cream cheese, powdered sugar and whipped topping; spread on cooled crust.
- Mix together blueberries, salt, lemon juice, sugar, water and cornstarch in small saucepan. Cook until thickened. Cool completely.
- Spread blueberry mixture on cream cheese layer.
- Refrigerate at least 4 hours before serving.

Trippin' On Persimmons

—from Sue Engle, Extension and Agricultural Information
         University of Missouri-Columbia

Sweet, date-like persimmons with their characteristic fresh tang have formed markers on a personal trail that meanders through time and space to my present home in Columbia.

Persimmons are linked with memories of red-gold-purple foliage afire on folded hills, and with family rituals of fall.

Like those who originally settled Missouri, I am an immigrant. When I moved to Missouri I brought with me, as a tangible memory, several cans of persimmon pulp, acquired at gourmet prices, to share with friends in Boone County.

To my chagrin, I learned that persimmons grow wild all over Missouri. Far from a gourmet treat, many farmers consider them a nuisance.

"Don't you make persimmon pudding and muffins and such?" I asked.

"Nope," was the laconic reply. "We feed 'em to the pigs."

Now pigs have many good points, but they are not well equipped to appreciate the delights of persimmon pudding. This state of affairs simply can't continue!

Persimmons are gathered in autumn, close to the time of the first hard frost. They are puckery and inedible if not completely ripe. Full mature, however, they are a rare treat.

The fruit needs lots of water to form and ripen, so watch for trees that have had a good source of water. The ones we use grow beside a runoff ditch and seem to have adequate moisture even in otherwise dry summers.

Gather persimmons dead ripe, after they fall to the ground. They will be quite soft. Discard any that are spoiled. Those with broken skin may be kept if not spoiled and if thoroughly rinsed. The fruit is fragile and must be processed immediately.

Remove stem ends. Process through a Foley food mill, sieve, or colander. Discard seeds and skins. Spoon pulp into tightly closed containers and freeze. Food processors and blenders are not recommended for preparation.

Persimmon Pudding

½ cup Mid-America Farms Butter
1 cup Missouri Persimmon Pulp
1 cup sugar
1 egg
½ cup Mid-America Farms Buttermilk or Sour* Milk
⅔ cup flour
1 tsp baking powder
1 tsp cinnamon
1 tsp vanilla
½ cup Mid-America Farms Sweet Cream
½ cup Missouri Dandy Black Walnuts, coarsely chopped

*Sour milk by adding 1½ tsp. vinegar. Let stand about 15 minutes, then add ½ tsp baking soda and stir until foamy.

- Place butter in 9"x9" pan and put in oven at low heat. It will be melted by the time you mix the other ingredients.

- Blend together pulp, sugar, egg and buttermilk.
- Sift together and add flour, baking powder and cinnamon.
- Blend in vanilla, cream and nuts.
- Remove butter from oven. Swish around pan to grease, then pour as much as possible into batter and mix well. Pour batter into pan.
- Bake at 350 degrees for 1 hour. It will puff up considerably as it bakes, then fall back. It will pull away from the sides of the pan when done.
- Serve warm or cold with whipped cream, vanilla ice cream or simple vanilla sauce.
- Serves 12-16.
- Recipe can be doubled for 9"x13" pan to serve 20-24.

Work with youth-at-risk has become a priority of the Missouri 4-H. Success of these efforts is demonstrated in the words of one who was helped.

Kim relates, "In 1986, I dropped out of 4-H because it wasn't 'cool'. I started to drink, experiment with drugs, and I did poorly in school. Luckily my 4-H leader had faith in me and helped me to realize that I didn't need to do those things to be accepted. Now, I'm back in 4-H and doing better than ever."

An old mill rises regally
beside a Missouri stream
the proud relic
of an earlier day,
and a quieter way of life.

The Missouri underground is honeycombed with more than 5,000 known caves.

Marvel Cave in Branson's Silver Dollar City is America's third largest cavern with a main Cathedral chamber that rises 20 stories high. It was first discovered by the Osage Indians who were greatly troubled by the strange noises that echoed deep within the earth, and they called it the "Devil's Den."

Crystal Caverns near Cassville is believed to have the largest variety of formations in the United States. Camdenton's Bridal Cave holds the record for number of underground weddings. Hannibal's Cameron Cave has a lantern tour. So does Fisher Cave near Sullivan. Springfield's Fantasy Caverns is large enough for jeep-drawn trams to drive through, passing delicate soda straw formations, massive columns, and elegant stone curtains in a subterranean world.

Fantasy World Caverns, at Lake Ozark, has Indian burials and a large underground lake. Sparta's Honey Branch Cave is marked by lime "coral" deposits. Indian Burial Cave at Osage Beach was the final resting place for Indians who lived in the Woodland Period, almost 2,000 years ago.

Jesse James, when he wasn't robbing banks and trains, hid out in Meramec Caverns near Stanton. Ozark Caverns at Linn Creek is famous for its "Angel Showers," streams of water that flow from stalactites. Noel's Ozark Wonder Cave has seven rooms of multicolored onyx formations. Bluff Dweller's Cave, also at Noel, features a museum of minerals and crystal fossils. And Boon Cave near Rocheport, boasting one of the largest natural openings in Missouri, has been kept in its primitive state.

Purple Cow©

1 cup Meramec Vineyards Concord Grape Juice *2 scoops (about ¾ cup) Hiland Vanilla Ice Cream*	• Mix in blender until smooth or place ice cream in a glass and pour juice over top. • Serves 1

©Copyright, Meramec Vineyards. 1989.

Just south and west of Jefferson City some 60 miles is the manmade Lake of the Ozarks, which curls, and twists like a New Year's streamer. The lake is the largest of its kind in the United States.

A phenomenon exists here which is not encountered in natural lakes, usually surrounded by cottonwoods, basswoods and willows. Spanish oaks, red and white oaks, walnuts, butternuts and shagbark hickories — all hardwood trees—grow right at the water's edge, imparting a special beauty to the Lake of the Ozarks.

Catawba Lace Sherbet

1 envelope of unflavored gelatin
¼ cup cold water
1½ cups sugar
3 cups Meramec Vineyard Catawba Grape Juice
1 cup fresh red plums, finely chopped
2 egg whites, stiffly beaten

- Mix gelatin and cold water in a saucepan.
- Mix in sugar and grape juice.
- Stir over medium heat until sugar and gelatin are dissolved.
- Chill until syrupy.
- Fold in plums.
- Pour mixture into a 2 qt freezer container and freeze until half frozen.
- Scrape frozen mixture into a bowl and beat until fluffy.
- Fold in the beaten egg whites.
- Replace in freezer and freeze until hard.
- Spoon into serving glasses and garnish with a few red seedless grapes.
- Serves 12.

It is in Washington, along the banks of the Missouri River, that the majority of the world's corncob pipes are made. From a special strain of corn developed by the University of Missouri, which grows large cobs, low stalks and a lot of grain, the makers of corncob pipes manufacture their amusing, yet functional, items.

The corncob pipes are amusing because a small portion are sold as specialty advertising items or to tourists as adornments for hillbilly hats.

They are functional because corncob pipes are gaining the respect of pipe smokers everywhere.

One of the country's own Five Star Generals was hardly ever photographed without one. Indeed, a special design for him, known as the "Mac," was developed because of him. And isn't it curious that the only President from Missouri, Harry S. Truman, for the first time in history fired the General of the Army, Douglas MacArthur, who smoked only corncob pipes from Missouri?

Strawberries with Quick English Sauce

½ cup light brown sugar
4 oz Bailey's Irish Cream Liqueur
1 qt Central Dairy Heavy Cream
2 tbsp vanilla extract and/or
2 tsp vanilla bean, chopped
½ cup cornstarch
¼ cup water
8 portions fresh Missouri Strawberries, Raspberries, Blueberries, or a combination of all three
nutmeg

- Melt brown sugar in saucepan.
- Remove from heat and add liqueur.
- Return to burner and ignite with match. Be careful.
- When flame goes out, add cream and vanilla. Mix cornstarch and water into paste.
- Bring to a simmer and thicken with cornstarch mixture.
- Cool to warm temperature; pour over strawberries and/or other fruit.
- Dust with nutmeg if desired.
- Serves 8.

Chocolate Satin Marbled Cheesecake

Crust:

1½ cups graham cracker crumbs
6 tbsp Daricraft Butter, melted
¼ cup sugar

To make crust:

- Combine crumbs, melted butter and sugar.
- Press onto bottom of 9 or 10 inch springform pan and bake 5 to 10 minutes in 350 degree oven. Cool.

Filling:

2 lbs Philadelphia Cream Cheese
¾ cup sugar
2 eggs
1 tsp vanilla extract
2 tbsp cornstarch
1 cup Mid-America Farms Sour Cream
4 oz Flavors of the Heartland Chocolate Satin Sauce, melted and cooled slightly

Topping:

4 oz Flavors of the Heartland Chocolate Satin Sauce, melted and cooled slightly

To make filling:

- Beat cream cheese until light and fluffy.
- Add sugar and eggs, beating well.
- Add vanilla and cornstarch.
- Fold in sour cream. Pour into prepared crust.
- Carefully pour Chocolate Satin Sauce on top of filling, making 2 circles, 1 close to outer edge and the other closer to the center. Using a knife, cut almost through the filling as if cutting the pan in 6 equal sections.
- Bake in 325 degree oven 1 hour.
- Turn oven off and leave cheesecake in the oven for 3 hours with the door slightly opened.
- For topping, pour the remaining Chocolate Satin Sauce over the cooled cheesecake and smooth with a spatula.
- Refrigerate 8 hours or overnight.
- Serves 12.

Cookies-N-Cream Pie

1 (18 oz) pkg Mrs. Alison's
Chocolate Cream Cookies,
crushed
⅔ cup butter, melted
1 jar Flavors of the Heartland
Chocolate Satin Sauce
½ gal Central Dairy Cookies-
N-Cream Ice Cream
½ lb chocolate almond bark,
melted

- Mix crushed cookies and melted butter.
- Pack mixture in buttered 9"x13" pan.
- Bake only 8 minutes at 375 degrees. Cool completely.
- Scoop and press down ½ of the ice cream.
- Drizzle chocolate sauce over ice cream.
- Scoop and press down second ½ of ice cream.
- Top with melted chocolate almond bark.
- Freeze at least 2 hours before serving.
  Note:
- This recipe works well with any ice cream, particularly peppermint.
- ½ of this recipe fits in an 8x8 pan.
- Mrs. Alison's Chips A-Plenty, Pecan Melt-A-Way or Toasted Coconut also work well.

Potato Chip Cookies

1 cup Daricraft Butter
1 cup sugar
1 egg yolk
2 cups flour
1 tsp vanilla
1 cup Country Cooked Potato
Chips, crushed

- Cream butter, sugar and egg.
- Add remaining ingredients. Blend well.
- Roll 1 tbsp of dough into ball and flatten.
- Bake at 350 degrees, 8-10 minutes or until lightly brown.

J.C. Penney was only eight years old when it became evident that he would one day no doubt be a merchant.

He had been told that he would have to pay for his own clothing, and the boy badly needed $2.50 to buy a pair of shoes. He ran errands, collected and sold junk, and invested his meager savings in a pig. J.C. Penney fattened it, sold it, and used his profits to buy more pigs. He earned money to feed them by carrying away his neighbors' swill and cleaning out their pails for them.

The boy had quite a business.

But his father made him give it up.

The neighbors had never complained when Penney only had one or two pigs. But now he had so many that the noise and the smell was beginning to disturb them.

His father told him, "We have close neighbors, son, and you as well as I must look after their rights."

It was a lesson he never forgot.

In time, J.C. Penney would build his whole business philosophy on the foundation of his father's words.

Company Rice Custard

½ cup Della Gourmet Rice
2 cups Fairmont Milk
¼ cup butter
3 eggs
¾ cup sugar
1 tsp vanilla
¼ tsp salt
2 cups Fairmont Milk
½ tsp nutmeg

- Cook rice in 2 cups milk in top of double boiler until rice is tender.
- Add butter.
- Beat together eggs, sugar, vanilla, salt and 2 cups milk.
- Add hot rice mixture and mix well.
- Pour into greased 2-quart casserole.
- Sprinkle with nutmeg.
- Bake in 350 degree oven for 50 minutes

Early innovations for 4-H programs revolved around agriculture, home economics and related areas. Once strictly rural, 4-H projects are now structured for youths in urban areas as well.

4-H programs involve adult participation to foster a closer relationship between parents and their children. Groups work together on constructive community projects.

Learning takes place through 4-H programs in schools, family programs, special events, camps, informal groups, educational television, etc. International programs have been adopted to exchange opportunities and activities.

The mission of 4-H is to help young people become self-directing, productive and contributing members of society.

1. Develop inquiring minds, an eagerness to learn and the ability to apply science and technology.

2. Learn practical skills, develop competencies and acquire knowledge.

3. Strengthen abilities to make intelligent decisions, solve problems and manage their own affairs in a fast-changing world.

4. Acquire positive attitudes toward self and a feeling of self-worth.

5. Develop their potential by seeking and acquiring educational and vocational experiences.

6. Improve skills in communication and self-expression.

7. Develop effective interpersonal relationships with adults and other youth.

8. Maintain optimum physical and mental health.

9. Develop concern for involvement in community and public affairs.

10. Increase leadership capabilities.

11. Develop socially acceptable behavior, personal standards and values for living.

12. Develop abilities to perform as productive, contributing citizens.

13. Use time wisely in attaining a balance in life (work, leisure, family, community and self).

Buyer's Guide

Bakery Products

Bagel Factory, St. Louis
Barker's (Barker's Honey Farm), Tina
Bunny (Lewis Brothers Bakery), Sikeston
Butternut, Boonville and Springfield
Colonial (Colonial Baking), Springfield
Fantasia Confections, Sedalia
Haas (Haas Baking), St. Louis
Hazelwood Farms (Petrofsky's Enterprises),
   Maryland Heights
Hostess (Continental Baking), Kansas City
James (James Pecan Farms), Brunswick
Kolb's (Royal Cheese Cakes), St. Louis
Nancy Ann (Schnuck Baking), St. Louis
Pet-Ritz (Pet), St. Louis
Petrofsky's (Petrofsky's Enterprises), Maryland Heights
Progresso (Pet), St. Louis
Schnuck's (Schnuck Baking), St. Louis
Shepherdsfield (Shepherdsfield Bakery), Fulton
Taystee (Taystee Baking), Kansas City
Wonder (Continental Baking), Kansas City

BBQ Sauce

Andy's (Andy's Seasoning), St. Louis
Cattlemen's (Durkee-French), Springfield
Char-B-Que (Athena Creations), St. Louis
J-Bar-J (J-Bar-J Bar-B-Q), Osage Beach
Louis Maull, St. Louis
Missouri Classic, Rolla
Missouri Country Kitchens, Unionville
Old Southern (Garden Compliment), Kansas City
Ott's (Ott Food Products), Carthage
The Good Life (Goodlife Ind.), Springfield
Wicker's (Wicker's Products), Hornersville

Beef

Ambassador Meat, Kansas City
Boyle's (Boyle's Famous Corned Beef), Kansas City
Gwinn's (Gwinn's Foods), St. Louis
Kansas City Steak Co. (Ambassador Meat), Kansas City
Mott (Mott Meat), Rockville
Nordic (Nordic Meats), Raymore
Old Kansas City Dry Aged Steaks (L & C Meat),
   Independence
Oscar Mayer, Columbia
Party Steak, Carthage
Ranch House (Diggs Packing), Columbia
Sweet Betsy's From Pike (Woods Smoked Meats),
   Bowling Green
Swiss (Swiss Processing Plant), Hermann
Tiger Packing, Columbia
Tiger Country (Diggs Packing), Columbia
Weber (Weber Meat Service), Freeburg
Wilson (Wilson Meat), Columbia
Wilson (Toppers Meat), Sedalia
Winter's (Winter's Meat Processing), Blue Springs

Beverages

Barrel (Speaco Foods), Kansas City
Excelsior Springs (Mineral Water Sys.), Excelsior Springs
IBC (IBC Root Beer), Hazelwood
Meramec (Meramec Vineyards), St. James
Missouri Gold (Gray's Creek Vineyard), Webster Groves
Ozark (Speaco Foods), Kansas City

Ozark Mountain Tea, Cape Girardeau
Purified Water (Unlimited Water Proc.), St. Louis
Time Out (Nicolay Enterprises), St. Louis
Vess (Vess Beverages), St. Louis

Candy

Bauer (Price Candy), Richmond
Blum's of San Francisco (Price Candy), Richmond
Bogdon (Bogdon Candy), Kansas City
Chase & Poe, St. Joseph
Classic Country Candies, Mt. View
Country Candy Corn, Warsaw
Fresh Way (Grubbs Products), St. Louis
Good and Plenty (Leaf), St. Louis
Good and Fruity Leaf), St. Louis
Hess Candy, Hume
James (James Pecan Farms), Brunswick
Merb's Candies, St. Louis
Midwestern Pecan, Nevada
Missouri Dandy (Hammons), Stockton
Osage (Osage Pecan), Butler
Price Candy, Richmond
Soisson's Confections, Sullivan
Stoll (Stoll Candies), St. Louis
Sunline (Sunmark), St. Louis
Sunmark, St. Louis
Twizlers (Leaf), St. Louis
Wing (Wing Candy), Branson
World of Candy, Lathrop

Charcoal

Kingsford, Belle
Lite-A-Bag (Nubbin Ridge), West Plains
Patio Chef, Meta
Presto (Imperial Products), Ellsinore
Royal Oak (Royal Oak Enterprises), Branson
Steakhouse (Imperial Products), Ellsinore

Cheese and Dairy Products

Bailey Farm (Bailey Farm Dairy), St. Louis
Baker's Cheese (Sanitary Dairy Foods), St. Louis
Central Dairy, Jefferson City
Dairy Sweet (Milnot), Seneca
Daricraft (Mid-America Dairymen), Springfield
Fairmont-Zarda Dairy, Kansas City
Glamour (Mid-America Dairymen), Springfield
Hiland (Hiland Dairy Foods), Springfield
Kraft (Kraft Foods), Springfield
Libby (Carnation/Nestle), Trenton
Mid-America Farms (Mid-America Dairymen), Springfield
Milnot, Seneca
Morningland Dairy, Mountain View
Pet, St. Louis
Pevely (Pevely Dairy), St. Louis
Prairie Farms (Prairie Farms Dairy), St. Louis
Progresso (Pet), St. Louis
Schreiber's (Perryville Cheese), Perryville
Sport Shake (Mid-America Dairymen), Springfield
Sunshine (Milnot), Seneca

Condiments

Accent (William Underwood, Div. of PET), St. Louis
Andy's Seasoning, St. Louis
Aunt Joan's Ozark Country Mustard

(Ozark Country Foods), Osage Beach
Aunt Nene's (Aunt Nene's Specialty Foods), Lucerne
Char Mustard (Athena Creations), St. Louis
Char-B-Que (Athena Creations), St. Louis
French's (Durkee-French Foods), Springfield
Goodman (Goodman Mfg.), Carthage
Herb Gathering, Kansas City
Heritage (Garden Compliments Old Southern),
  Kansas City
Hummingbird Hills, Ashland
Meyer (Meyer Horseradish), St. Louis
Old Southern (Garden Compliments Old
  Southern), Kansas City
Ott's (Ott Food Products), Carthage
Ozark Botanicals, Dixon
Passport Seasonings (J & D Passport
  Seasonings), Columbia
Riverbluff (Riverbluff Farm), Owensville
Rogers (Speaco Foods), Kansas City
Missouri Country Kitchens, Unionville
Silver Springs (Meyer Horseradish), St. Louis
Spicecraft, St. Louis
Stephenson's (Stephenson's Old Apple
  Farm Restaurant), Lee's Summit
Wishbone (Thomas Lipton), Independence

Cookies and Crackers

Amber & Company Telecookies, Independence
Dad's (Dad's Cookie), St. Louis
Mrs. Alison's (Mrs. Alison's Cookie), St. Louis
Spring Hollow (Spring Hollow Cookie), Springfield
22nd Street (Imperial Baking), St. Louis

Desserts, Frozen

A & W (Merritt Foods), Kansas City
Bailey Farm (Bailey Farm Dairy), St. Louis
Banquet (ConAgra Frozen Foods), Macon
Belefonte (Belefonte Ice Cream), Kansas City
Central Dairy, Jefferson City
Chapman, St. Louis
Circle D (Chapman Ice Cream), St. Louis
Country Pride (ConAgra Frozen Foods), Macon
Country Fresh (Chapman Ice Cream), St. Louis
Dairy Queen (Gold Bond Ice Cream of Missouri), Sikeston
Disney (Gold Bond Ice Cream of Missouri), Sikeston
Dole (Merritt Foods), Kansas City
Drumstick (Ice Cream Specialties), St. Louis
Eskimo Pies (Merritt Foods), Kansas City
Eskimo Pie (Ice Cream Specialties), St. Louis
Fresh Way (Grubbs Products), St. Louis
Gelati Gandolfo, St. Louis
Good Humor (Gold Bond), Sikeston
Heath (Ice Cream Specialties), St. Louis
Hiland, Springfield
Holy Cow (Odessa Ice Cream), Odessa
Merritt (Merritt Foods), Kansas City
North Star (Ice Cream Specialties), St. Louis
Odessa (Odessa Ice Cream), Odessa
Pevely (Pevely Dairy), St. Louis
Prairie Farms (Chapman Ice Cream), St. Louis
Sweetheart (Chapman Ice Cream), St. Louis

Fish

Country Fresh Catch, Moberly
Catfish Corner (Lambrich Fisheries), Imperial
Mountain Springs (Mountain Springs
  Trout Farm), Highlandville
Party Steak, Carthage

General Foods

Aunt Jemima (Quaker Oats), St. Joseph
Della Gourmet Rice (Flavors of the Heartland), Columbia
Edmond's (Edmond's Chile), St. Louis
Fleischman's (Nabisco Brands), St. Louis
Golden Dipt, St. Louis
Gwinn's (Gwinn's Foods), St. Louis
Heartland (PET), St. Louis
Hillbilly (D-V Bean House), Lampe
Hodge's (Hodge's Chili), St. Louis
Hodgson Mill (Hodgson Mill Enterprises), Gainesville
Kraft (Kraft Foods), Springfield
Lentils Divine, St. Louis
Lil Guy (Lil Guy Foods), Kansas City
Menu Master (Int'l Dehydrated Foods), Monett
Nabisco (Nabisco Brands, USA), Carthage
Nature's Sprouts, St. Louis
Old El Paso (PET), St. Louis
Progresso (PET), St. Louis
Quaker (Quaker Oats), St. Joseph
Shepherdsfield (Shepherdsfield Bakery), Fulton
Stephenson's (Stephenson's Old Apple
  Restaurant), Lee's Summit
22nd Street (Imperial Baking), St. Louis
Walker's (Walker's Food Products), North Kansas City

Fruits and Vegetables, Preserved

Aunt Nene's (Aunt Nene's Specialty Foods), Lucerne
Old Tyme (Berger Foods), St. Louis
Rogers (Speaco Foods), Kansas City
Stephenson's (Stephenson's Old Apple
  Farm Restaurant), Lee's Summit

General Sauces

Allen Pride (Halben Food Mfg.), St. Louis
Chef Mate (Carnation/Nestle), Trenton
Flavors of the Heartland (Chocolate Satin), Columbia
French's (Durkee-French), Springfield
Heritage (Garden Compliment Old Southern),
  Kansas City
Jose Espinosa (Walsh Food), Jefferson City
La Casita (La Casita Homestyle Mexican
  Food), Holts Summit
Lasco (Halben Food Mfg.), St. Louis
Louisa (Louisa Food Products), St. Louis
Old El Paso (PET), St. Louis
Old Southern (Garden Compliment Old
  Southern), Kansas City
Ott's (Ott Food Products), Carthage
Persimmon Hill (Persimmon Hill Berry Farm), Lampe
Rogers (Speaco Foods), Kansas City
Sally Mountain (Missouri Country Kitchens), Unionville
Soisson's Confections, Sullivan
Temptor (Halben Food Mfg.), St. Louis
V's (V's Restaurant), Independence

Honey

Barker's (Barker's Honey Farm), Tina
Dean Sims (Dean Sims Honey), Sweet Springs
Gibbons (Gibbons Bee Farm), Ballwin

Jams, Jellies and Preserves

Aunt Hazel's (Willis/Elliott), Spickard
Aunt Mollie's (Aunt Mollie's Old Time Foods), Kirbyville
Aunt Nene's (Aunt Nene's Specialty Foods), Lucerne
Centennial Farms, Augusta

East Wind's (East Wind Community), Tecumseh
James Country, Liberty
Log Cabin Artistry, Kearney
Persimmon Hill (Persimmon Hill Berry Farms), Lampe
Stephenson's (Stephenson's Old Apple Farm
   Restaurant), Lee's Summit

Meats, Processed

Alma (Alma Coop Locker), Alma
Alewel's (Alewel's Country Meats), Warrensburg
Ambassador Meat, Kansas City
Armour, Kansas City
Boyle's (Boyle's Famous Corned Beef), Kansas City
Burger's (Burger's Ozark Country Cured Hams), California
Chef Mate (Carnation/Nestle), Trenton
Country Butcher Shop, Palmyra
Farmland Foods, Kansas City
Frick's (Frick's Meat Products), Washington
G & W (G & W Meat and Bavarian Style Sausage),
   St. Louis
Grandpa A's (Alewel's Country Meats), Warrensburg
Irish Gold (Ambassador Meats), Kansas City
Libby (Carnation/Nestle), Trenton
Little Dixie (Moberly Packing), Moberly
Menu Master (International Dehydrated Foods), Monett
Max German, St. Louis
Oldani Brothers (Oldani Brothers Sausage), St. Louis
Oscar Mayer, Columbia
Park Avenue (Kaw Valley Meat), Independence
Perry County (Perry County Meats), Perryville
Ranch House (Diggs Packing), Columbia
Ranch Wood (Moberly Packing), Moberly
Scavuzzo (Ambassador Meat), Kansas City
Seitz (Seitz Foods), St. Joseph
Shaw Farms (Shaw Farms Meat Processing), Hawk Point
Sweet Betsy From Pike (Woods Smoked Meats),
   Bowling Green
Swiss (Swiss Processing Plant), Hermann
Tiger Packing, Columbia
Tiger Country (Diggs Packing), Columbia
Uncle Tom's (Ozark Country Foods), Osage Beach
Underwood (William Underwood, Div. of Pet), Hannibal
Volpi (Volpi and Company), St. Louis
Weber (Weber Meat Service), Freeburg
Williams Bros. (Williams Bros. Meat), Washington
Wilson (Toppers Meat), Sedalia
Wilson (Wilson Foods), Marshall
Wilson (Wilson Meat), Columbia

Nuts

Byrd's Pecans, Butler
David & Sons, St. Louis
Eagle Brand (Anheuser Busch), St. Louis
East Wind's (East Wind Community), Tecumseh
Guy's (Guy's Foods), Liberty
James (James Pecan Farms), Brunswick
Midwestern Pecan, Nevada
Miller Farms Pecans, De Witt
Missouri Dandy (Hammons Products), Stockton
Mound City (Mound City Shelled Nut), St. Louis
Osage Pecan, Butler

Oils and Vinegars

Creamo (PVO Foods), St. Louis
Herbal Design (Flavors of the Heartland), Columbia
High Score (PVO Foods), St. Louis
Hollywood (Pet), St. Louis
Inland Products, Carthage

Mikado (PVO Foods), St. Louis
Ozark (Speaco Foods), Kansas City
Passport Seasonings (J & D Passport Seas), Columbia
Progresso (Pet), St. Louis
Riverbluff (Riverbluff Farm), Owensville
Rogers (Speaco Foods), Kansas City
Speas (Speaco Foods), Kansas City

Pasta

Hodgson Mill (Hodgson Mill Enterprises), Gainesville
La Bella (American Italian Pasta), Excelsior Springs
Louisa (Louisa Food Products), St. Louis
Mangia Italiano, St. Louis
Masterchoice (American Italian Pasta), Excelsior Springs
R & F (Ravarino and Freschi), St. Louis

Popcorn

Angel Fluff, Golden City
Country Candy Corn, Warsaw
Fancy Farms, Bernie
Old Vienna (Old Vienna Snacks), St. Louis
Popcorn Plus, Savannah
Popcorn World, Trenton
Prairie Poppins, Gallatin
Pro-Popt, Bernie

Pork

Alewel's (Alewel's Country Meats), Warrensburg
Baumgartner (Baumgartner Boone County Cured
   Hams), Rocheport
Burger's (Burger's Ozark Country Cured
   Hams), California
Corn King (Wilson Foods), Marshall
Country Butcher Shop, Palmyra
Double G (Double G Brands), St. Louis
Farmland Foods, Kansas City
Frick's (Frick's Meat Products), Washington
Grandpa A's (Alewel's Country Meats), Warrensburg
Gwinn's (Gwinn's Foods), St. Louis
Irish Gold (Ambassador Meat), Kansas City
Kretschmar (Kretschmar Brands), Concordia
Little Dixie (Moberly Packing), Moberly
Max German, St. Louis
Miller Ham, St. Louis
Nordic (Nordic Meats), Raymore
Old Kansas City (L & C Meat), Independence
Old Missouri (Kretschmar Brands), Concordia
Oscar Mayer, Kirksville
Party Steak, Carthage
Ranch Wood (Moberly Packing), Moberly
Roundtree (Kretschmar Brands), Concordia
Seitz (Seitz Foods), St. Joseph
Shaw Farms (Shaw Farms Meat Processing), Hawk Point
Sweet Betsy From Pike (Woods Smoked Meats),
   Bowling Green
Swiss (Swiss Processing Plant), Hermann
Tiger Packing, Columbia
Volpi (Volpi and Company), St. Louis
Weber (Weber Meat Service), Freeburg
Williams Bros. (Williams Bros. Meat), Washington
Wilson (Wilson Foods), Marshall
Wilson (Wilson Meat), Columbia
Wilson (Toppers Meat), Sedalia
Winkler's (Boone County Hams), Columbia
Winter's (Winter's Meat Processing), Blue Springs

Poultry

Blue Ribbon (Simmons Industries), Southwest City
Burger's (Burger's Ozark Country Cured Hams), California
ConAgra Turkey, Carthage
Honeysuckle (Cargill), California
Hudson (Hudson Foods), Dexter, Noel and Springfield
Medallion (Cargill), California
Menu Master (International Dehydrated Foods), Monett
Oscar Mayer, Columbia
Paramount (Cargill), California
Party Steak, Carthage
Queen Esther (Queen Esther Food), St. Louis
Riverside (Cargill), California
Ro Jo (Ro Jo Farms), West Plains
Show-Me (John's Produce), Campbell
Sweet Betsy From Pike (Woods Smoked Meats),
  Bowling Green
Swiss (Swiss Processing Plant), Hermann
Town & Country (Simmons Industries), Southwest City
Tyson (Tyson Foods), Monett and Neosho

Processed Foods, Frozen

Armour Star (ConAgra Frozen Foods), Macon
Banquet (ConAgra Frozen Foods), Macon, Marshall
  and Milan
Chefmaster (ConAgra Frozen Foods), Marshall
Country Pride (ConAgra Frozen Foods), Macon
Hazelwood Farms (Petrofsky's Enterprises),
Maryland Heights
Kids Cuisine (ConAgra Frozen Foods), Marshall
Louisa (Louisa Food Products), St. Louis
Lucia's Pizza, Kirkwood
Morton (ConAgra Frozen Foods), Marshall
Mr. Dell's (Mr. Dell Foods), Kearney
Ozark Valley (ConAgra Frozen Foods), Marshall
Party Steak, Carthage
Petrofsky's (Petrofsky's Enterprises), Maryland Heights
Quelle Quiche, St. Louis
Ringo Foods, Kansas City
Shepherdsfield (Shepherdsfield Bakery), Fulton
Tiger Packing, Columbia
Winter's (Winter's Meat Processing), Blue Springs

Snack Foods

Backer's (Backer's Potato Chip), Fulton
Country Candy Corn, Warsaw
Country Cooked (Country Cooked Potato Chips),
  Memphis
Eagle Brand Snacks (Anheuser/Busch), St. Louis
Guy's (Guy's Foods), Liberty
Hallams (SSI), Nixa
La Casita (La Casita Homestyle Mexican Foods),
  Holts Summit
Old Vienna (Old Vienna Snacks), St. Louis
Rold Gold (Rold Gold Foods), St. Louis
Sommer's (Sommer's Food Products), Salisbury
SSI, Nixa

Spirits

Bardenheier Winery, St. Louis
Bias Vineyard, Berger
Blumenhof Vineyards, Dutzow
Boone Country Winery, Defiance
Bristle Ridge Vineyards, Knob Noster
Bud Light (Anheuser/Busch), St. Louis
Budweiser (Anheuser/Busch), St. Louis
Busch (Anheuser/Busch), St. Louis

Busch Light (Anheuser/Busch), St. Louis
Bynum Winery, Lone Jack
Carver Wine Cellar, Rolla
Cedar Ridge Winery, Augusta
Eckert's Sunny Slope Winery, Washington
Ferrigno Vineyard & Winery, St. James
Heinrichshaus Vineyards and Winery, St. James
Hermannof Winery, Hermann
King Cobra (Anheuser/Busch), St. Louis
L.A. (Anheuser/Busch), St. Louis
Les Bourgeois Winery & Vineyard, Rocheport
McCormick (McCormick Distilling), Weston
Michelob (Anheuser/Busch), St. Louis
Mission Creek Winery, Weston
Montelle Vineyards, Augusta
Mount Pleasant Winery, Augusta
Mount Pleasant Winery, Abbey Vineyard, Cuba
Natural Light (Anheuser/Busch), St. Louis
O'Vallon Winery, Washburn
Ozark Vineyards, Chestnutridge
Peaceful Bend Vineyards, Steelville
Pirtle's Weston Vineyards, Weston
Reis Winery, Licking
Sainte Genevieve Winery, Ste. Genevieve
Spring Creek Winery, Blue Springs
St. James Winery, St. James
Stone Hill Winery, Hermann
Winery of the Little Hills, Inc., St. Charles

Index

Sandwiches

Main Dishes

Beef

Pork

Rabbit

Lamb

Chicken

Turkey

Seafood

Pasta

199

Take Home the Taste of Ott's

SAVE 55¢ when you choose any 16 oz. size or larger Ott's Dressing or Barbecue Sauce

This coupon good toward the purchase of:

110943

- Ott's Chef-Style FAMOUS Dressing
- Ott's Reduced Calorie, Low Sodium FAMOUS Dressing
- Ott's Chef-Style ITALIAN Dressing
- Ott's Ozark Maid BUTTERMILK Dressing
- Sweet-n-Mild Barbecue Sauce
- Barbecue Sauce
- Smoky Barbecue Sauce

5 41423 15055 7

TO THE CONSUMER: This coupon can be redeemed only with the purchase of the brands specified. Coupon cannot be transferred or exchanged. Any other use constitutes fraud. TO THE RETAILER: We will reimburse you for the face value of this coupon plus 8¢ handling provided that you and the consumer have complied with the terms of our coupon offer. This coupon is good only when redeemed by you from a consumer at thime of purchase. The consumer must pay any sales tax involved. This coupon is non-assignable. Invoices proving purchase of sufficient stock to cover coupons presented must be shown upon request. For redemption mail to: Ott Food Products, P.O., Box 880651, El Paso, Texas 88588-0651. Cash value of 1/20 of 1¢. Void where taxed, prohibited or restricted by law. LIMIT ONE COUPON PER PURCHASE.

Take Home the Taste of Ott's
55¢

SAVE 55¢ when you choose any 16 oz. size or larger Ott's Dressing or Barbecue Sauce

This coupon good toward the purchase of:

110943

- Ott's Chef-Style FAMOUS Dressing
- Ott's Reduced Calorie, Low Sodium FAMOUS Dressing
- Ott's Chef-Style ITALIAN Dressing
- Ott's Ozark Maid BUTTERMILK Dressing
- Sweet-n-Mild Barbecue Sauce
- Barbecue Sauce
- Smoky Barbecue Sauce

5 41423 15055 7

TO THE CONSUMER: This coupon can be redeemed only with the purchase of the brands specified. Coupon cannot be transferred or exchanged. Any other use constitutes fraud. TO THE RETAILER: We will reimburse you for the face value of this coupon plus 8¢ handling provided that you and the consumer have complied with the terms of our coupon offer. This coupon is good only when redeemed by you from a consumer at thime of purchase. The consumer must pay any sales tax involved. This coupon is non-assignable. Invoices proving purchase of sufficient stock to cover coupons presented must be shown upon request. For redemption mail to: Ott Food Products, P.O., Box 880651, El Paso, Texas 88588-0651. Cash value of 1/20 of 1¢. Void where taxed, prohibited or restricted by law. LIMIT ONE COUPON PER PURCHASE.

Take Home the Taste of Ott's
55¢

SAVE 55¢ when you choose any 16 oz. size or larger Ott's Dressing or Barbecue Sauce

This coupon good toward the purchase of:

110943

- Ott's Chef-Style FAMOUS Dressing
- Ott's Reduced Calorie, Low Sodium FAMOUS Dressing
- Ott's Chef-Style ITALIAN Dressing
- Ott's Ozark Maid BUTTERMILK Dressing
- Sweet-n-Mild Barbecue Sauce
- Barbecue Sauce
- Smoky Barbecue Sauce

5 41423 15055 7

TO THE CONSUMER: This coupon can be redeemed only with the purchase of the brands specified. Coupon cannot be transferred or exchanged. Any other use constitutes fraud. TO THE RETAILER: We will reimburse you for the face value of this coupon plus 8¢ handling provided that you and the consumer have complied with the terms of our coupon offer. This coupon is good only when redeemed by you from a consumer at thime of purchase. The consumer must pay any sales tax involved. This coupon is non-assignable. Invoices proving purchase of sufficient stock to cover coupons presented must be shown upon request. For redemption mail to: Ott Food Products, P.O., Box 880651, El Paso, Texas 88588-0651. Cash value of 1/20 of 1¢. Void where taxed, prohibited or restricted by law. LIMIT ONE COUPON PER PURCHASE.

Take Home the Taste of Ott's
55¢

SAVE 55¢ when you choose any 16 oz. size or larger Ott's Dressing or Barbecue Sauce

This coupon good toward the purchase of:

110943

- Ott's Chef-Style FAMOUS Dressing
- Ott's Reduced Calorie, Low Sodium FAMOUS Dressing
- Ott's Chef-Style ITALIAN Dressing
- Ott's Ozark Maid BUTTERMILK Dressing
- Sweet-n-Mild Barbecue Sauce
- Barbecue Sauce
- Smoky Barbecue Sauce

5 41423 15055 7

TO THE CONSUMER: This coupon can be redeemed only with the purchase of the brands specified. Coupon cannot be transferred or exchanged. Any other use constitutes fraud. TO THE RETAILER: We will reimburse you for the face value of this coupon plus 8¢ handling provided that you and the consumer have complied with the terms of our coupon offer. This coupon is good only when redeemed by you from a consumer at thime of purchase. The consumer must pay any sales tax involved. This coupon is non-assignable. Invoices proving purchase of sufficient stock to cover coupons presented must be shown upon request. For redemption mail to: Ott Food Products, P.O., Box 880651, El Paso, Texas 88588-0651. Cash value of 1/20 of 1¢. Void where taxed, prohibited or restricted by law. LIMIT ONE COUPON PER PURCHASE.

55¢/2

55¢/2

Save 55¢
on any two cans

PROGRESSO®
Soup

A8116

11128

5 41196 11128 1

55¢/3

55¢/3

Save 55¢
when you buy any three cans

UNDER WOOD
Meat Spreads

11000

5 47800 11000 8

55¢/2

55¢/2

Van de Kamp's
frozen seafoods
Buy any two packages

Save 55¢

A8116

970370

5 19600 11128 8

55¢/1

55¢/1

Save 55¢
when you buy one

HOLLYWOOD ™

Oil/24 oz. or larger

70005

5 70005 11055 9

BERRY
CONNECTION

BLUEBERRIES ❧ *RASPBERRIES* ❧ *GOOSEBERRIES*

Larry, Linda & Scott Jones
417/862-1094

50¢ per gallon discount with coupon

ROUTE 4 • BOX 688 • SPRINGFIELD, MO 65802
I-44 to exit 70, one-half mile north on B

STEINBAUGH BLUEBERRY FARM

Art and Juanita Steinbaugh
Route 1, Box 244
Billings, Mo. 65610

50¢ off per gallon with this coupon

Located 4 miles east of Billings, Mo. on 14 Hwy.
or 12 miles west of Nixa, Mo. on 14 Hwy.

417-744-2045

SAVE 55¢

EXPIRES DEC. 31, 1990

ON TWO-BAG PURCHASE

SAVE 55¢

Quick Cooking HASH BROWNS *AND/OR* **Quick Cooking COUNTRY CHUNKS**

Mr. Grocer, please redeem this coupon by sending to: Mr. Dell Foods, Inc., P. O. Box 880391, El Paso, Texas 88588-0391. You will be paid 55¢ plus 8¢ handling. Invoices proving purchase of stock to cover coupons redeemed must be furnished on request. Cash redemption value 1/20th cent. This coupon good only on brand specified. Offer limited to one coupon per purchase. Coupon void if copied, or where prohibited by law.

© 1990 Mr. Dell Foods, Inc. Kearney, Mo. 64060

75947 100675

55¢ Take Home the Taste of Ott's 55¢

SAVE 55¢ when you choose any 16 oz. size or larger Ott's Dressing or Barbecue Sauce

This coupon good toward the purchase of:

110943

- Ott's Chef-Style FAMOUS Dressing
- Ott's Reduced Calorie, Low Sodium FAMOUS Dressing
- Ott's Chef-Style ITALIAN Dressing
- Ott's Ozark Maid BUTTERMILK Dressing
- Sweet-n-Mild Barbecue Sauce
- Barbecue Sauce
- Smoky Barbecue Sauce

5 41423 15055 7

55¢ Take Home the Taste of Ott's 55¢

SAVE 55¢ when you choose any 16 oz. size or larger Ott's Dressing or Barbecue Sauce

This coupon good toward the purchase of:

110943

- Ott's Chef-Style FAMOUS Dressing
- Ott's Reduced Calorie, Low Sodium FAMOUS Dressing
- Ott's Chef-Style ITALIAN Dressing
- Ott's Ozark Maid BUTTERMILK Dressing
- Sweet-n-Mild Barbecue Sauce
- Barbecue Sauce
- Smoky Barbecue Sauce

5 41423 15055 7

55¢ Take Home the Taste of Ott's 55¢

SAVE 55¢ when you choose any 16 oz. size or larger Ott's Dressing or Barbecue Sauce

This coupon good toward the purchase of:

110943

- Ott's Chef-Style FAMOUS Dressing
- Ott's Reduced Calorie, Low Sodium FAMOUS Dressing
- Ott's Chef-Style ITALIAN Dressing
- Ott's Ozark Maid BUTTERMILK Dressing
- Sweet-n-Mild Barbecue Sauce
- Barbecue Sauce
- Smoky Barbecue Sauce

5 41423 15055 7

Please send me a copy (copies) of THE NEVER ENDING SEASON at a special price of $16.95 plus $2.50 for shipping and handling.

$16.95 X ___copies: $ _____

plus $2.50/copy: $ _____

Total $ _____

Enclosed is my check, payable to Missouri 4-H Foundation, 212 Whitten Hall, Columbia, MO 65211

Name: _____

Address: _____

City/State/Zip: _____

Please send me a copy (copies) of THE NEVER ENDING SEASON at a special price of $16.95 plus $2.50 for shipping and handling.

$16.95 X ___copies: $ _____

plus $2.50/copy: $ _____

Total $ _____

Enclosed is my check, payable to Missouri 4-H Foundation, 212 Whitten Hall, Columbia, MO 65211

Name: _____

Address: _____

City/State/Zip: _____

Please send me a copy (copies) of THE NEVER ENDING SEASON at a special price of $16.95 plus $2.50 for shipping and handling.

$16.95 X ___copies: $ _____

plus $2.50/copy: $ _____

Total $ _____

Enclosed is my check, payable to Missouri 4-H Foundation, 212 Whitten Hall, Columbia, MO 65211

Name: _____

Address: _____

City/State/Zip: _____